Walking and Exploring the

Southern Broads

By Joe Jackson

All maps provided are OS OpenData with additions. It is recommended to take a detailed up-to-date map of the area with you whilst on a walk. Public Footpaths are generally well waymarked but there are areas which may require some basic map reading skills.

For walks and video guides for hundreds of routes all over Great Britain then visit:

www.walkinginthewild.co.uk

While every effort is made by myself to ensure the accuracy of this guidebook before going to print, changes can occur during the lifetime of an edition. It is recommended that you check local information like public transport, shops and accommodation if any of these will be required prior to starting any walk or holiday. Even rights of way can be altered over time.

Please keep to the countryside code by being safe, plan ahead and follow any signs. Leave gates and property as you find them. Protect plants and animals by taking litter home. Keep dogs under close control and please be considerate to other people.

Front Cover: Strumpshaw Fen (Walk 9)

About the Author

Joe's passion for walking began as a small child, being taken out amongst the marshes, reedbeds and woodlands of the Norfolk Broads to see the local wildlife and develop a passion for the great outdoors. This blossomed in the early 2010s with a temporary move to a stunning location surrounded by the Lakeland Fells. Being out in the mountains on a near daily basis led to developing a walking blog website that still runs to this day and has been adapted into a more comprehensive database.
Visit: www.walkinginthewild.co.uk

Along with this was the development of a YouTube Channel and the creation of walking videos following national trails, long distance footpaths, mountain routes, moorlands and open countryside. A natural progression to this was to begin creating guidebooks for some of the spectacular places that were visited. So began the first long distance walk guidebook in the form of the Little Ouse Path. From there on more and more guidebooks have been produced to help visitors get the most out of the great outdoors.

Contents

The Broads National Park
An overview of England's most important wetland

The Broads National Park is formed of a series of mostly navigable rivers and lakes (known as Broads) that together, with the surrounding marshland, create the largest protected wetland in the country. Home to dozens of very rare species of wildlife including Bittern, Crane, Bearded Tit and the Swallowtail Butterfly, there are numerous nature reserves to explore within the national park boundary. Within its 117 square miles there are also three long distance trails as well as countless miles of marsh and riverbank walking. The Broads were formed from peat excavations in the middle ages and as sea levels began to rise these diggings became flooded, and now many hundreds of years later provide the delicate habitat we see today.

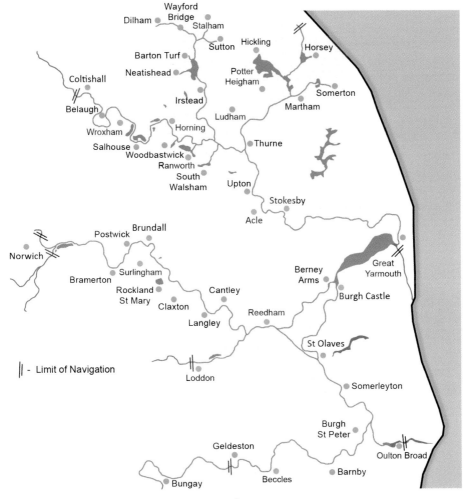

Understanding the Maps and Icons

At the start of each chapter are a selection of icons at the bottom of the page which allow for a brief overview of what is offered at the town or village. These icons indicate the following:

| Convenience Store | Mooring | Pub | Eatery | Pharmacy | Nature Reserve | Historic Interest |

The maps included in this book are provided by Ordnance Survey OpenData VectorMap® with additions that most visitors may find useful such as footpaths, pubs and restaurants, public transport links, points of interest, parking and mooring. Please be aware that some places may charge for moorings (especially outside public houses) but this is sometimes offset if you are using their services. Signs should be in place stating the charge or whether it is 24 hour free mooring. Car Parking is also included on the map as a blue 'P' of which there may be a small charge. Boatyards have also been added to aid pleasure cruisers to additional facilities such as pump outs and drinking water.

Public Footpaths

Point of Interest

Train Station

Public House

Moorings

Bridge (With Height)

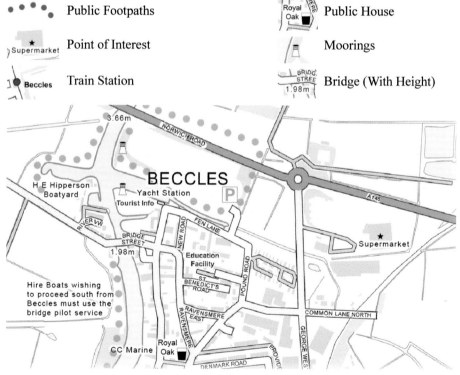

Holidaying on the Broads

The Broads National Park is most famous for being a holiday destination for boat enthusiasts with over 200km (120 miles) of navigable waterways. The seven main rivers within the national park are the River Waveney, Thurne, Bure, Chet, Yare, Ant and Wensum which connect together along with 63 broads (lakes) to form one of the largest wetlands in the UK. Naturally with all this water around most visitors choose to take in the sights from the river and either book a fully equipped motor cruiser or yacht. To see the entire area a minimum of one week is recommended due to tidal restrictions at Breydon Water which can prevent access to the southern or northern broads and rivers. Holidaying on the Broads has been around for decades with many well established marinas offering various craft for hire and have been around for nearly 100 years! Whether it be a back to basics type of holiday or state of the art luxury cruiser, there's something for every budget and taste. For those who want to take things a little slower then seeing areas of the Broads from the adventurous position of a Kayak or Canoe is highly recommended, accessing areas other boaters cannot reach and being at one with the river and wildlife. If sailing the rivers is not for you then there are plenty of B&Bs, Caravan and Campsites and riverside cottages dotted around the Broads providing the perfect base to venture out on foot or bicycle. There are literally hundreds of miles of footpath and bridleways in and around the Broads National Park taking walkers to hidden viewpoints and wildlife hot-spots that simply cannot be accessed by boat or car. With almost 100 walks in this book ranging from less than 1 mile and up to 8 miles exploring riverbank, reedbed, woodland, marsh and even beach dunes proves there is so much more to see than you may first realise.

Acle

River Bure

Barnby (Cove Staithe)

Barnby is a small village just off the A146 Beccles to Lowestoft Road which has largely merged with the parish of North Cove. Most of the village, along with The Swan Inn, Garden Centre and Cafe sit just along the main road, about a 30 minute walk from Cove Staithe which provides the nearest available mooring. Nestled between the A146 and the River Waveney is Barnby Broad and the North Cove Nature Reserve, the latter being owned and managed by Suffolk Wildlife Trust and home to lots of interesting flora and fauna.

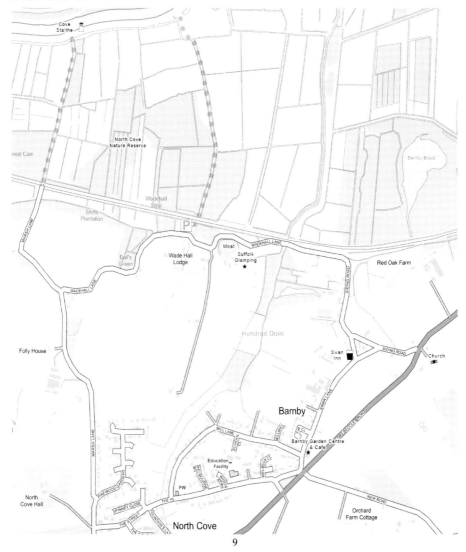

Walk 1:	Distance: 6.3km (3.9 Miles)
Barnby Circular	**Time:** 2 Hours
	Parking: Village Car Park **NR34 7QG**

From Cove Staithe, follow the path south just opposite the moorings to the right. After just over 500m the track crosses the railway line onto Marsh Lane and continue along the lane up to the junction close to Low Farm. Turn left along the winding road called Wadehall Lane and follow the lane for 650m where you will encounter a small car park and footpath on the left. This is where you would start the walk if arriving by car. Continue a little further along the road looking for a footpath on the right heading south along a track beside a property. At the split just ahead keep left and continue through the gate along the field edge heading south. After passing one field the path follows the edge of another and then bends to the left into the village of Barnby via a narrow alley between houses. Turn left along the road up to the junction with the garden centre and cafe directly ahead. Turn left and follow the road to the split next to the Swan Inn and bear right. Follow the road round to the right and up to the A146 bypass.

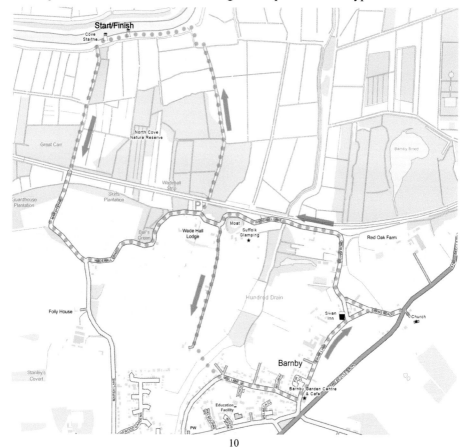

Wade Hall Moated Site

The moat alongside Wade Hall is fairly substantial and remains water filled on its northern side. The moat likely enclosed the Manor of Wathe or Wade Hall which was thought to be in this area around the 12th Century. Nothing upstanding remains of the hall but some archaeologists have suggested that the size and shape of the moat may indicate the site was actually a Norman Ringwork, a type of castle built during the 11th and 12th Centuries.

The church of St John the Baptist is down a trackway opposite and once visited, backtrack along this road and at the junction bear right. At the next junction bear right again along Sidings Road which is followed for 1km to the small car park by the footpath you encountered earlier. Turn right to follow the path north across the railway line and after about 700m you will arrive at an open grazing field and a gate. Head through the gate and follow the edge of the field on the left up to another gate onto the riverbank path with Cove Staithe about 400m over to the left.

Wade Hall Moat

11

The Swan Inn

St John The Baptist

The parish church of St John The Baptist dates from the 13th Century with a 14th century tower and the remains of three 15th century wall paintings inside. The building has been given a Grade II* listing.

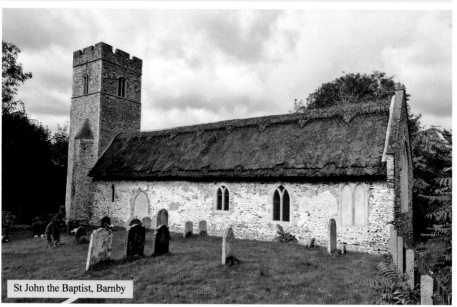

St John the Baptist, Barnby

North Cove Nature Reserve

The North Cove Nature Reserve is a lovely small reserve with several hides overlooking pools, woodland and marsh. The reserve is maintained entirely by volunteers who complete conservation work every Wednesday.

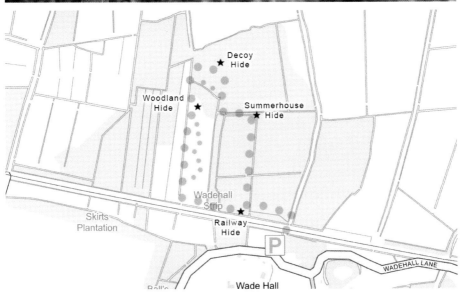

Beccles

River Waveney

Beccles

Beccles is the most southerly town in The Broads National Park and is actually just across the border into Suffolk. The staithe offers plenty of 24 hour free moorings and there is a large car park nearby (free for first 2 hours). Boaters should be aware that Beccles Old Bridge has a clearance of 1.98m at low tide and advice should be sought prior to navigation and the pilot service must be used. The town centre offers visitors a choice of shops, pubs and restaurants, too many to show on the map. There are plenty of walks in the area that take in the atmosphere of the Southern Broads including visiting Beccles Marsh Nature Reserve and villages like nearby Gillingham and Geldeston. The town is well connected with good public transport links to Lowestoft and Ipswich, with additional connecting trains to Norwich and regular bus services to Great Yarmouth.

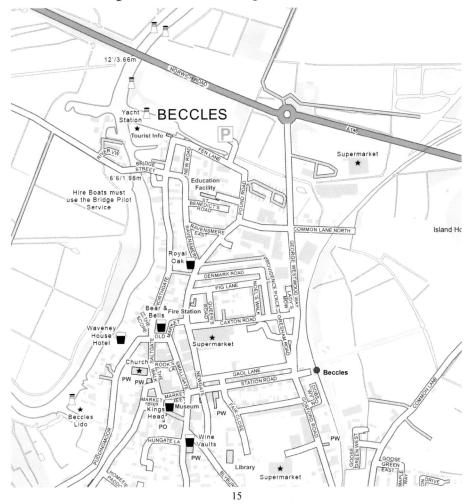

St Michael's Church, Beccles

Beccles Church is quite unique in the fact that its bell tower is completely separated from the main church. Its construction was finished in 1540 and stands 97ft high, and when open you can gain access to the top to see the spectacular view across the Norfolk and Suffolk countryside.

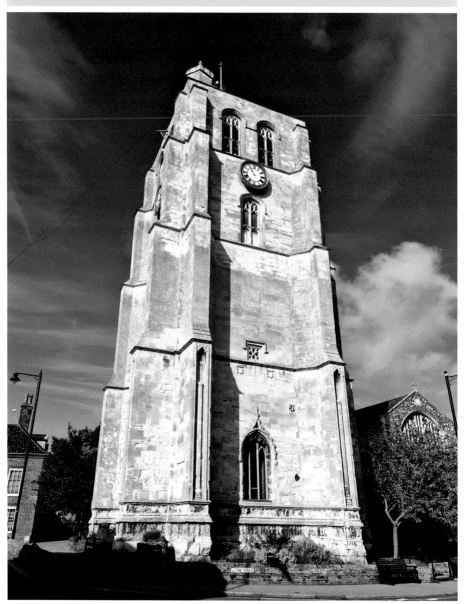

Walk 2: The River Waveney	Distance: 6.5km (4.0 Miles) Time: 2 Hours Parking: Staithe Car Park NR34 9BB

Starting off at Beccles Staithe follow Fen Lane south towards the town centre for 100 metres and turn right over Beccles Old Bridge. Continue along the road for 1.1km to the first left turn for 'The Street' in Gillingham. Continue 100m down The Street and take the first road on the left. Continue along this road as it meanders its way towards the river. After 1.1km there is a public footpath on your left. This is the hamlet of Dunburgh and consists of just a couple of houses but was likely historically more significant. A Roman burial was found here in the mid 19th Century with old OS Maps listing the top of the hill as the site of a possible Roman Camp although there is no other evidence of the camps existence. Follow the path on the left briefly next to the old railway line, and then along the River Waveney to the left. The riverbank footpath is now followed for 2.9km all the way back to Beccles Old Bridge where you can retrace your steps back to The Quay and Staithe along the road.

Beccles Old Bridge

The River Waveney at Beccles

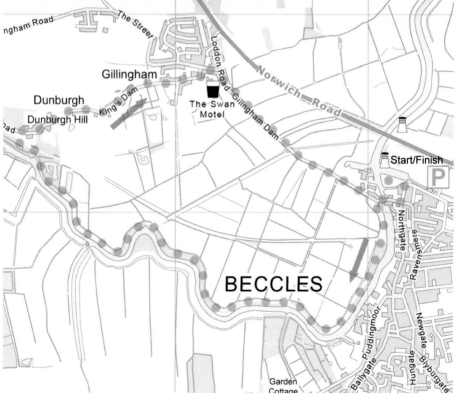

ngham Road
The Street
Gillingham
Loddon Road
Norwich Road
Dunburgh
King's Dam
Gillingham Dam
Dunburgh Hill
The Swan Motel
oad
Start/Finish
P
Northgate
Ravensmere
BECCLES
Puddingmoor
Ballygate
Newgate
Hungate
Blyburgate
Garden Cottage

Walk 3:
Gillingham

Distance: 6.9km (4.3 Miles)
Time: 2 Hours
Parking: Staithe Car Park   **NR34 9BB**

Beginning at Beccles Staithe, follow Fen Lane south towards the town centre for about 100m to Beccles Old Bridge which is on your right. Cross the bridge and follow the road for a little under 250m to a public footpath which is on your right. Follow the path around the boatyard and join the riverbank path. Follow this riverbank path north along the River Waveney and under the bypass flyover. Continue a further 1km along the riverbank to Boathouse Hill Cottages where the footpath continues across and up a field to join a track behind the cottages. Follow the track away from the river and through the farm to its entrance. Just as you leave the farm there is a track on the left. Head along this track for 650m where the path turns left and heads south along field edges and turns west to skirt the marshes. The path eventually arrives at the main road where you need to cross with care and follow the path on the opposite side which continues to a road.

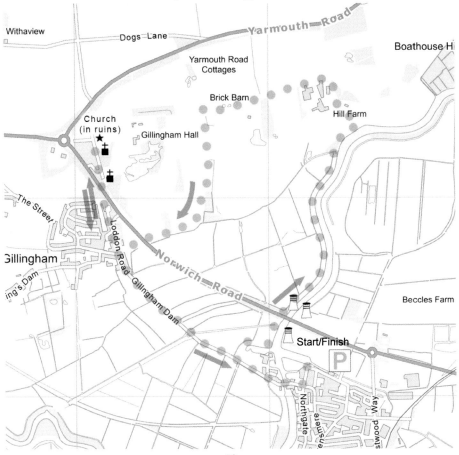

19

St Mary's Church, Gillingham

Upon arrival at the minor road you have the option of a detour to the three churches near Gillingham Hall which have been included in the distance and time for this walk. Turn right and follow the road for just over 100m to a road on the left. Turn down here and immediately right onto Forge Grove. Continue to the end of the where there is a footpath leading over a footbridge. At the other end the track joins a minor road which runs alongside the three churches. Once you have visited the churches you need to backtrack over the footbridge to Forge Grove. Turn left back onto Loddon Road and turn right heading south east into Beccles, turning left down Fen Lane back to the Staithe.

Ruins of All Saints, Gillingham

Beccles Marsh Nature Reserve

Beccles Marsh is home to some beautiful and rare wildlife including Kingfishers, Marsh Harriers and the Norfolk Hawker Dragonfly. There are numerous paths that can be taken around the marshes to complete shorter or longer circular walks with benches dotted around to enjoy the views. The map below shows the trails through the reserve.

River Waveney along Beccles Marsh

Berney Arms

River Yare

Berney Arms is one of the most remote locations in the Broads National Park, with access only by foot, train or boat. It sits just to the south west of Breydon Water and one of the last places to moor up before crossing the tidal estuary. Sadly the Pub closed its doors in 2015 with the nearest shops and pubs being in Reedham or across the river at Burgh Castle. The only other buildings at Berney Arms is the nearby windmill which is the tallest in Norfolk, a local farm which is used by the RSPB and a small train station with an infrequent service. 24 hour free moorings are available at the staithe. With few public footpaths in the local area the two walks provided in this chapter are both linear walks that make use of public transport.

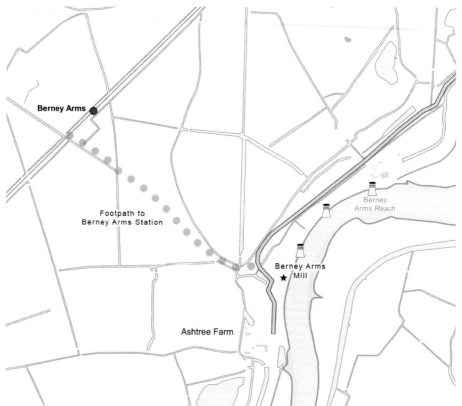

Berney Arms Mill

Berney Arms Mill was built in 1865 is one of the most famous mills in Norfolk. Standing at 71ft over the surrounding marsh, it's the tallest drainage mill on the Broads and protected as a scheduled ancient monument under the care of English Heritage.

Berney Arms Mill

Ensure you have checked the train times for the return journey as they stop very infrequently at Berney Arms station. Parking is available at the end of the walk.

From the moorings at Berney Arms, keep the river on the right and follow the riverbank footpath past the old Berney Arms Pub to the north east. The path follows the edge of Breydon Water for some way to a track at Breydon Pump and then back up onto the bank past Lockgate Drainage Mill. The bank path continues along the edge of Breydon Water for 3km until it arrives right next to the railway line. The path is sandwiched between the railway and the edge of Breydon Water and then moves away round a series of pools and back towards the railway line. The path follows the line of the railway for a short way and then moves away towards an RSPB Bird Hide which overlooks the vast expanse of Breydon Water. Continue along the riverbank path under Breydon Bridge and past the Supermarket Car Park to the train station just beyond on the left.

Breydon Water

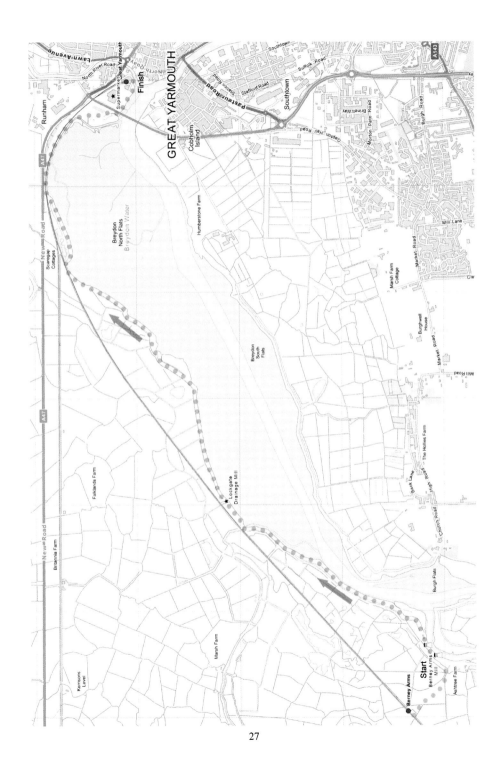

27

Walk 5: **River Yare Linear**	**Distance:** 8.3km (5.2 Miles) **Time:** 2 Hours 30 Minutes **Parking:** Staithe Car Park **NR13 3TE**

Ensure you have checked the train times for the return journey as they stop very infrequently at Berney Arms station.

From the moorings at Berney Arms, head left past Berney Arms Mill along the riverbank path to the south. The path passes Ashtree Farm and meanders for 3km to Cadges Mill and Polkey's Mill close to Seven Mile House. Stick to the riverbank path for a further 2.8km south west around several gentle curves to arrive at the edge of Reedham. The path runs parallel to a track and then descends off the bank to the road. Turn left along Holly Farm Road which heads north west over the railway line and up to a junction. Turn left down School Hill to the quay and turn right along the staithe. At the other side the road starts to head away from the river and at the junction ahead turn left. Follow the road round to the right and along a straight section towards reedham Train Station. At the junction the station is just over to the right by the bridge.

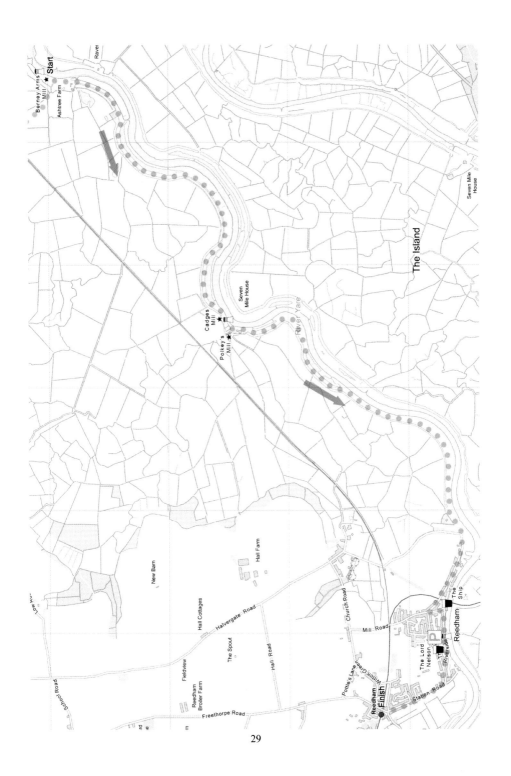

Start

Berney Arms
Mill

Ashtree Farm

Raver

The Island

Seven
Mile House

Cadges
Mill

Polkey's
Mill

River Yare

Seven Mile
House

New Barn

Hall Farm

Hall Cottages

Halvergate Road

Fieldview

The Spout

Hall Road

Reedham
Broiler Farm

Freethorpe Road

School Road

Low Rd

Church Road

Mill Road

Pottle's Lane

Wilton Green

Station Road

The Lord
Nelson

Riverside

The
Ship

Reedham

Reedham
Finish

Bramerton

River Yare

Bramerton

Bramerton is a small village on the south side of the River Yare close to the city of Norwich. It has a large staithe that extends in front of the village pub and a small parking area for cars. The large field by the staithe is the perfect place to enjoy outdoor games for visitors with free mooring and parking directly alongside. The Water's Edge is the only pub in the village and only place offering any amenities as sadly there is no longer a village shop, with mooring for customers directly outside as it overlooks a stunning section of the river.

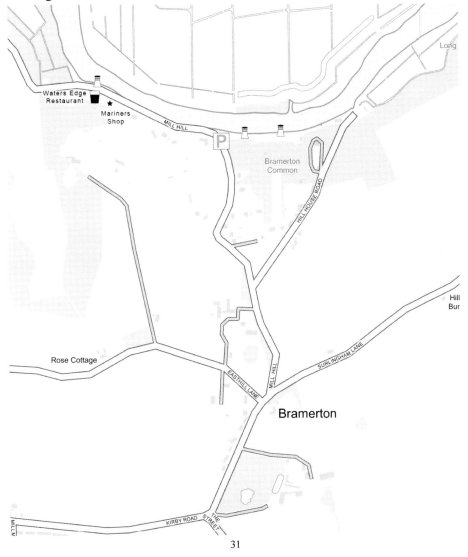

From Bramerton staithe, keep the river on the right and follow the road past the Water's Edge Restaurant and continue along this lane for a little over 1.5km (almost a mile). The road will arrive at a fork where you need to keep right into the village of Kirby Bedon. After a series of bends the road arrives at the two churches in Kirby Bedon, one being in use and the other ruined. Head back along the road in the direction of Bramerton and at the fork keep right this time along East Hill Lane. After approximately 900m there is a footpath on the left just before a house which heads north, eventually to a road where a right turn will lead back to Bramerton staithe.

Bramerton Staithe

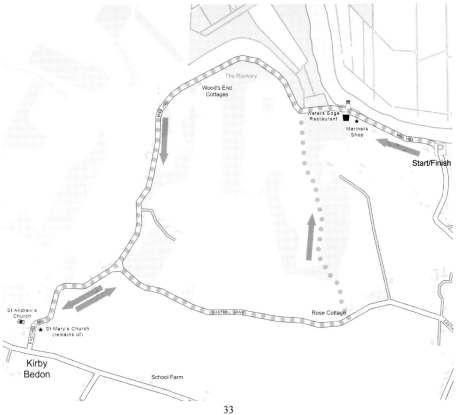

The Two Churches at Kirby Bedon

The twin churches of Kirby Bedon provide an interesting historical feature to walk to from Bramerton Staithe with both given a Grade II* listing. The oldest of the churches is St Mary's which dates to the 13th Century and sits in ruins within its own church yard and slowly crumbling since it was abandoned around 1700. Opposite is St Andrew's Church which dates to the 14th Century and still serves the small community.

The ruins of St Mary's Church, Kirby Bedon

Walk 7: Bramerton Circular	**Distance:** 3.1km (1.9 Miles) **Time:** 1 Hour **Parking:** Staithe Car Park　　　**NR14 7ED**

From Bramerton Staithe cross the green to the fence on the far side of the mooring area where a gate leads onto a public footpath. The path follows the fence up to a driveway (Hill House Road) where you need to turn right and follow this to the lane and up to the junction. Turn left and follow the lane up to the junction ahead. Turn right and then right again along Easthill Lane and after about 500m there is a public footpath on the right along a track next to a house. Follow the track north to eventually arrive at the road and the bear right leading past the Waters Edge Restaurant and to Bramerton Staithe.

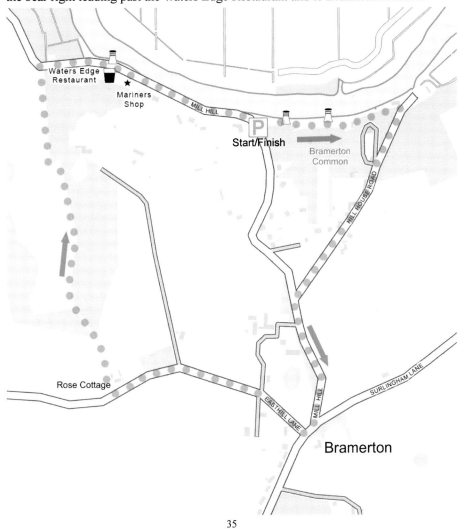

The Waters Edge, Bramerton

Brundall

River Yare

Brundall

Brundall is a large village along the River Yare famous for its boat building history. There's plenty of free moorings and parking for visitors with a couple of shops, cafes and takeaways along the main street including the Ram Inn and The Yare. Brundall has excellent transport links with regular train journeys to Norwich and Great Yarmouth as well as a regular bus service from the high street. Locally there are a couple of nature reserves, one being Church Marsh and located just a few minutes from the main high street, and the other being RSPB Strumpshaw Fen which offers several miles of trails, a visitor centre and numerous hides overlooking acres of reedbed and broad. It is also one of the best sites in Norfolk to see Bearded Tits and the elusive Bittern.

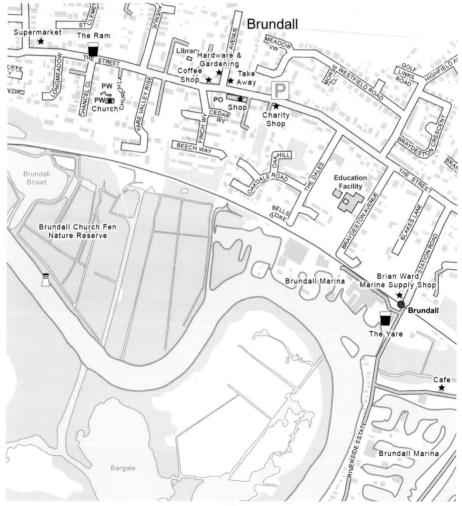

Brundall Church Fen Nature Reserve

Brundall Church Fen is a small nature reserve covering just 6.9 acres, with a short circular walk providing access to free moorings along the River Yare. The reserve is home to plenty of wildlife species including Woodpeckers, Water Voles and occasionally Otters. Access to the fen is along Church Lane and over the railway crossing or from the moorings directly alongside.

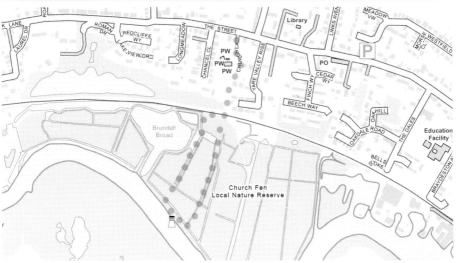

Church Fen Moorings

Boardwalk through Church Fen

From Brundall train station, follow station road towards the village and turn left along The Street. Shortly ahead turn right down Highfield Avenue and about 50m past Nurseries Avenue a footpath branches off to the right. Continue along the fences to the road and along the path opposite. The path arrives at a field and follows the left hand edge up to St Michaels and All Angels church.

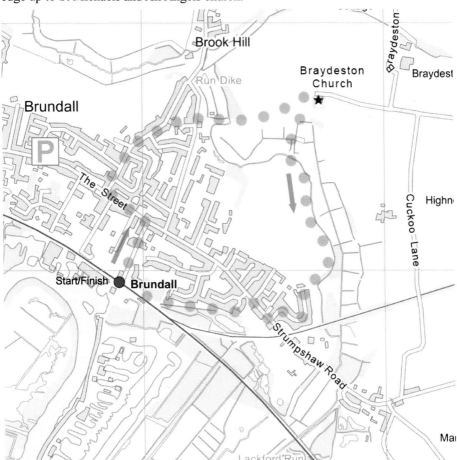

Head back onto the road and turn left, and then left again, south through the grazing field and up to the field boundary ahead. Turn left along the field edge and shortly the path arrives at St Michaels Way cul-de-sac. Follow St Michaels Way to the junction and then turn right. Just past the bus stop on the other side of the road is a public footpath that heads through the trees and back to the train station.

St Michael's Church, Braydeston

The solitary church of St Michael is a stunning Grade 1 listed building dating to 1440 with the potential for an older church being on the site prior to this, as some parts appear to be 12th or 13th Century. St Michael is actually the parish church for Braydeston, now a deserted medieval village with no visible remains.

Note that the distance and time above is to the reserve entrance and back, and does not include walking any of the trails at Strumpshaw Fen so allow extra time for this.

Beginning from Brundall train station take the public footpath on the right by the railway crossings, signposted to RSPB Strumpshaw Fen. Follow the path up to the road and turn right along Strumpshaw Road for 650m, under the railway bridge and up Stone Road with a brown sign for the RSPB Reserve. Turn right again along Low Road and just after the bend in the road there is a footpath on the right just before a house. Cross the field to the track and turn left, following the track parallel to the railway line and up to the road. The entrance to the reserve is just on the right across the railway crossing. The return follows the same route back to Brundall.

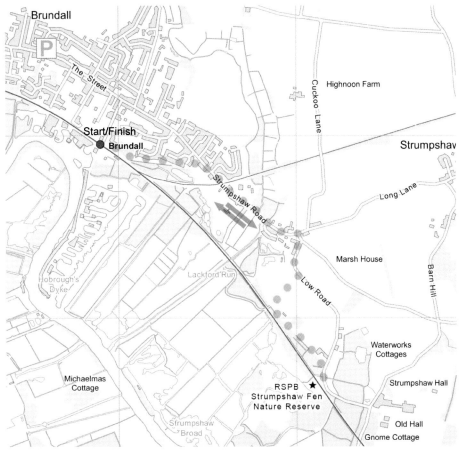

RSPB Strumpshaw Fen

Strumpshaw Fen is a spectacular nature reserve managed by the RSPB and open to visitors from dawn till dusk. The reserve is home to some of the rarest wildlife in the country including Bitterns, Marsh Harriers and Bearded Tits so the binoculars and camera are a must! Several miles of trails and numerous bird hides means it's possible to spend an entire day here with light refreshments available at the main reception. There is free entry for RSPB Members with a small charge for other visitors and free parking on site.

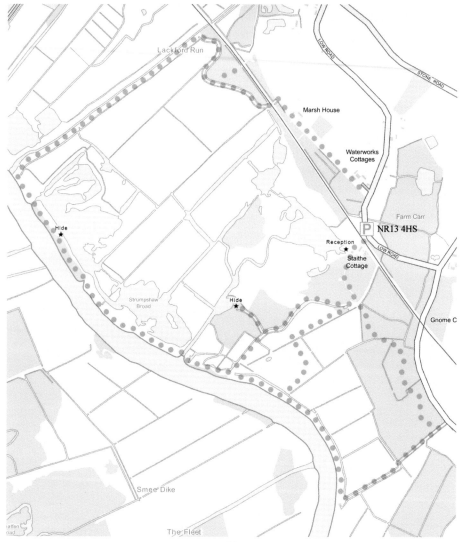

RSPB Strumpshaw Fen

Bungay

River Waveney

Bungay

Bungay is a market town on the edge of the Broads National Park and the only place included in this book without any moorings due to the river being unnavigable beyond Geldeston a few miles down stream. The town is believed to have originated in Saxon times and developed further into the Norman period. Around 1100AD Bungay Castle was built with the natural curve of the River Waveney providing a defence on the northern and western side. There are plenty of amenities, with numerous pubs and restaurants around the town centre and some lovely countryside to explore and good public transport links into Beccles.

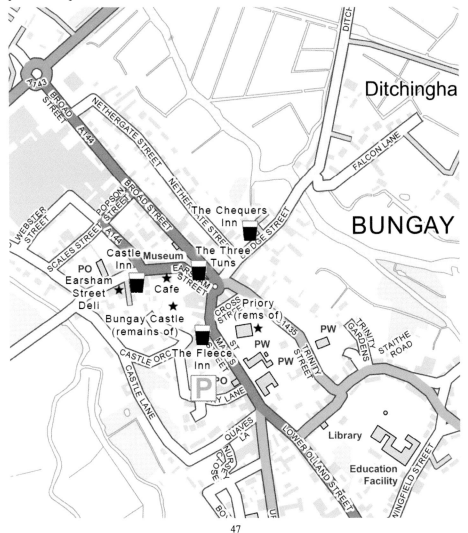

Bigod Castle, Bungay

Bungay Castle was originally built as a Motte and Bailey around 1100AD and from the mid-12th Century, stone fortifications were added. The ruins of the curtain wall, gatehouse and keep are free to explore and protected as a Grade I listed building.

St Mary and the Priory Ruins

The church of St Mary in the centre of town is one of two churches in the local area and the Priory Church on an ancient Benedictine Convent founded in 1183. Part of the priory ruins remain in the church yard and are free to explore. The church has been given a Grade I listing.

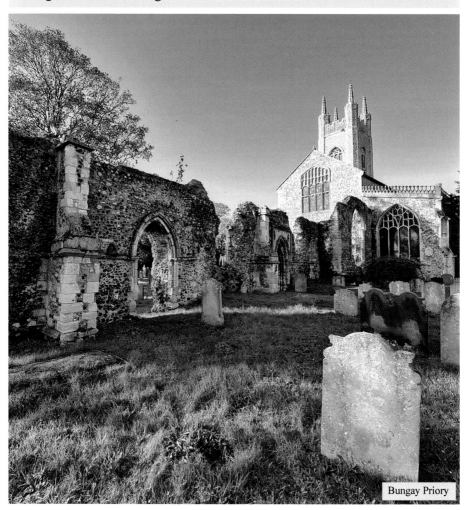

Bungay Priory

Holy Trinity Church, Bungay

The Grade 1 listed Church of the Holy Trinity is just across the road from St Mary's Church and potentially pre-dates the castle and priory. The round tower of the church is reputed to be Saxon in origin although this has not been confirmed and could be early Norman.

Walk 10:
Bungay Town

Distance: 1.2km (0.75 Miles)
Time: 45 Minutes
Parking: Town Car Park   **NR35 1DB**

From the town centre parking, head west towards the park which shows off some of the earthworks from the nearby Castle. Follow the road north along Castle Orchard and bear left up a wide alley to the spectacular castle ruins. Just past the ruins is a narrow alley running north past The Castle Inn and to Earsham Street. Turn right and follow the road as it bends round to the right and up to Butter Cross (see next page). Continue south past Butter Cross and St Mary's Church is just on the left. Cross the church yard past the Priory Ruins to Trinity Street and turn right to the Holy Trinity Church. Follow the road south and bear right along Wharton Street and at the end of the road turn right. Follow the road towards the Catholic Church but just before, turn left along Priory Lane, signposted to the Parking, and follow it to the car park.

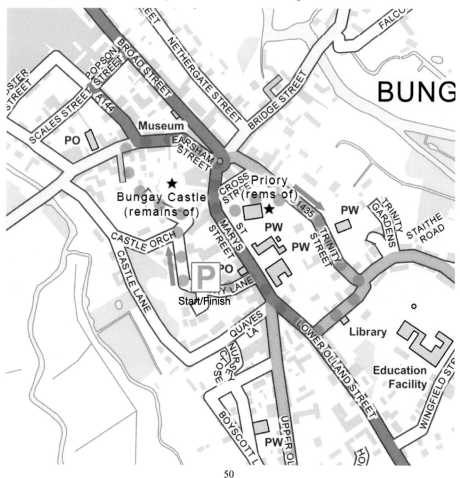

Butter Cross

In the central marketplace sits Butter Cross, an octagonal dome dating to 1689. The Grade I listed building was constructed where local farmers displayed their farm produce and butter, hence the name.

From Priory Lane Car Park head out onto the lane and turn right and follow the road round to the right. Bear right again and then turn left in front of Jesters coffee shop to the castle ruins and at the far side follow the alley up to the road. Turn right and follow the road up to the junction and turn left along Bridge Street. The road passes the Chequers Inn, heads over the River Waveney and along Ditchingham Dam. After about 400m there is a public footpath on the right through a metal gate across grazing meadows to the east. The path approaches buildings and turns right along a line of hedges then diagonally to the road. Turn right and follow the road for 1km up to the road junction and turn left along the main road (ignore Low Road). Take care along here but after just 150m there is a path on the right (Angles Way). The path crosses fields up to the road and continues straight ahead picking up the path at the other side of the sharp bends between hedgerows. At the road the Angles Way continues just over to the right and gently bends to the right, sticking between hedge-lines and eventually arrives at the road. Turn right and follow the road past Mettingham Castle and at the fork bear left along New Road. At the junction turn left again and after just over 200m there is a public footpath on the right.

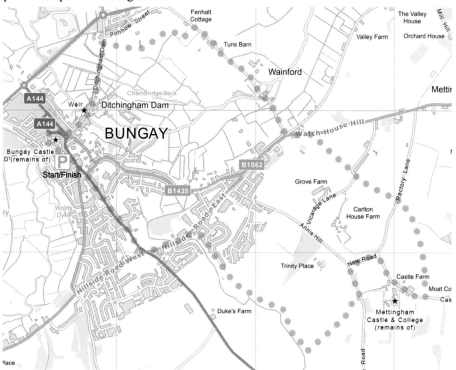

Follow the path south west for about 550m to the bottom of the field where there is a dike. Turn right and follow the dike north west and at the fork keep left where the path eventually arrives at a gate and onto Meadow Road. follow the road to the junction and turn left and just round the corner there is a path on the left along a track towards a house where the path heads along the left side to the road. Turn left and at the junction turn right back into the town of Bungay. Opposite the St Edmund's Primary School is Priory Lane and the car park.

River Waveney at Ditchingham Dam

Mettingham Castle

Mettingham Castle is a fortified manor house close to the town of Bungay and dates to 1342. From 1394 it was given to a college of secular canons from Norton who established themselves within the castle grounds and continued until the dissolution of the monasteries in 1542. Most of the castle was demolished in the 18th Century and what remains has been protected with a Grade II* listing.

Mettingham Castle

Norfolk County Council

Footpath

The Angles Way

Public Footpath

Norfolk Trails

Dog Walkers

Dogs must be kept on a lead at
all times along the boardwalk and
footpath adjacent to Glebe Marshes.

Pathmakers

Burgh Castle

River Waveney

Burgh Castle

Burgh Castle is a beautiful historic village famous for its spectacular and exceptionally well preserved Roman Walls and lovely views over Breydon Water. The village has a small post office, two pubs and a take away, with the nearest food shop being around 2 miles down the road in nearby Belton. The countryside around Burgh Castle is largely agricultural with the northern side bordering the vast Breydon Water and the River Waveney to the west. Burgh Castle, along with Berney Arms on the opposite side of the river provide the last two opportunities for boaters to stop as Breydon Water can only be crossed at certain times of the day due to the tide.

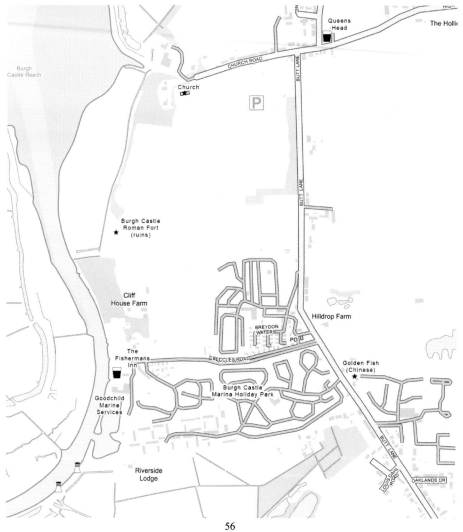

Burgh Castle Roman Fort

The Roman Fort at Burgh Castle is believed to have been constructed between 240 - 280 AD and one of a number of shore forts along the Norfolk Coast, with one just a few miles north at Caister-on-Sea and another at Brancaster. What makes the fort at Burgh Castle so special is the fantastic level of preservation of the outer defensive wall which still stands at its original height of almost 5 metres. Sadly the western wall collapsed into the River Waveney long ago but the northern, eastern and southern walls are almost complete. A civilian settlement known as a 'Vicus' grew up around the fort's northern, eastern and southern sides and survives as crop marks on the ground. The site was then believed to have been used as a pre-conquest monastery although no archaeological evidence has ever been found to prove its true location. In the late 11th or early 12th Century a Motte and Bailey castle was also built in the south western corner which was completely destroyed in 1839.

<table>
<tr><td>

Walk 12:

The Roman Fort

</td><td>

Distance: 3.5km (2.2 Miles)
Time: 1 Hour
Parking: Village Car Park   **NR31 9QG**

</td></tr>
</table>

From the moorings just south of the boatyard, follow the Angles Way north east towards the boatyard and away from the river. Turn left, continuing along the Angles Way opposite the house and along the edge of the marina and boatyard. Turn left to the Fisherman's Inn and along the Angles Way riverbank path. Soon the path turns right, away from the River Waveney and towards the site of the Roman Fort. Do not go up to the fort just yet, instead turn left along the edge of the marsh and follow this path, keeping the trees on the right, until you reach a track close to a farm. Turn right along the track and follow it to the church of St Peter and St Paul. Follow the track south past the church and just after the church yard there is a gate into a field on the right and a split in the path. Keep left along the diagonal path leading to another gate and across the next field up to the spectacular Roman Fort. After exploring the fort exit along the south western end back down to the Angles Way and backtrack along the same path along the River Waveney to the moorings. This walk can also be started from Burgh Castle car park.

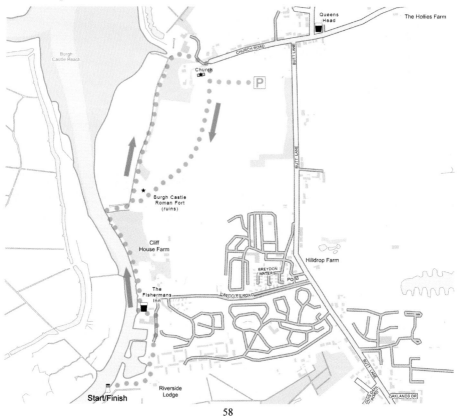

St Peter and St Paul, Burgh Castle

The Grade II* listed church of St Peter and St Paul sits close to the Roman Fort on its northern side with origins dating to the late 11th Century. The church is one of only 124 round tower churches in Norfolk and retains its interesting 13th Century character.

Walk 13: **Breydon Water**	**Distance:** 9.0km (5.6 Miles) **Time:** 3 Hours **Parking:** Village Car Park **NR31 9QG**

Transport back to the start is required on this walk by either Bus or Taxi.

This linear walk to Great Yarmouth begins at the mooring south of the boatyard with an optional start from the village car park and can be joined close to the church. From the moorings just south of the boatyard, follow the Angles Way north east towards the boatyard and away from the river. Turn left, continuing along the Angles Way opposite the house and along the edge of the marina and boatyard. Turn left to the Fishermans Inn and along the Angles Way riverbank path. Soon the path turns right, away from the River Waveney and towards the site of the Roman Fort where you need to turn left along the edge of the marsh and towards a track.

River Waveney

Turn left continuing along the Angles Way riverbank path which curves round and follows the edge of Breydon Water. Several gates are passed through along the edge of Breydon Water and its roughly 4.5 miles until you pass under the A47 overpass and towards the houses on the edge of Great Yarmouth. The path joins Breydon Road, continue to the end and turn left along Lady Haven Road and just ahead turn right along the narrow walkway to the road just ahead. Turn left along Steam Mill Lane which progresses up to the main road by Haven Bridge. Cross Haven bridge and turn right up to the town hall and then left up Regent Street. Follow the road round to the right along a short section of King Street and then left into Regent Road. Just ahead on the left is the entrance to Market Gates shopping centre and alongside is the bus station.

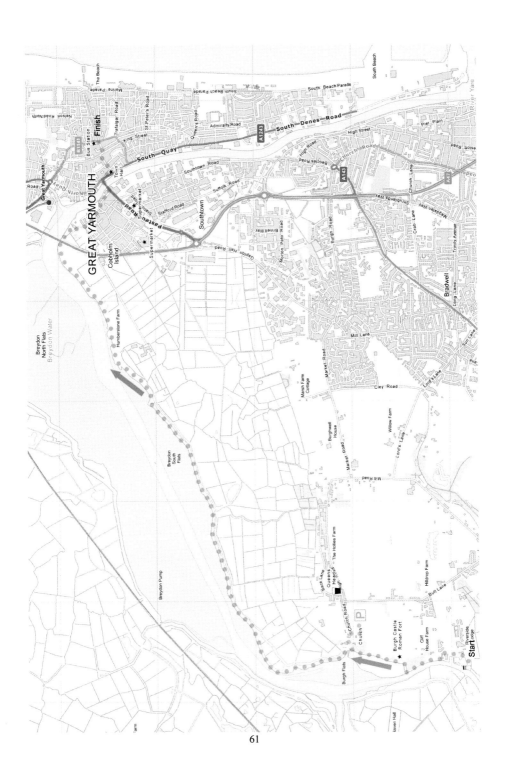

Burgh St Peter

River Waveney

Burgh St Peter

Burgh St Peter has a sparse population that covers a large geographical area. The main village is set back from the River Waveney with most amenities located at the Waveney River Centre including the Waveney Inn, a small convenience store and canoe and boat hire. Just north of the River Centre is the village church with its unusual stepped tower and about 2 miles west of here is the White Lion pub in Wheatacre. The village used to have two mills with only one surviving in the village centre.

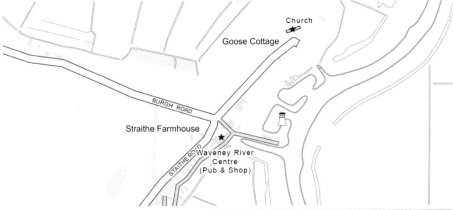

Burgh St Peter Staithe

Waveney River Centre

The Waveney River Centre is a real hub of activity along the River Waveney and offers visitors overnight accommodation, with hotel rooms and camping, the Waveney Inn, moorings, boat hire and a small convenience store.

St Mary's Church, Burgh St Peter

St Mary's Church in Burgh St Peter is an interesting church just north of the Waveney River Centre. Originally dating to the 12th Century there have been numerous additions and alterations through the years, namely the adding of a unique 'ziggurat' style tower in the 18th Century. The church has been given a Grade II* listing.

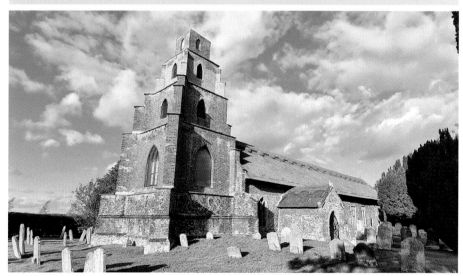

From the staithe in Burgh St Peter head onto the road and turn left. Follow Staithe Road for approximately 1 mile to a split, keep left here along Grays Road and follow it until the junction 1km ahead. At the junction turn right and follow the lane into Burgh St Peter, past the Mill and up to the crossroads. Continue along the road opposite and up to New Buildings Farm where there is a public footpath on the right. The path heads down the farm track and up to a gate by a brick barn, head through and bear left then right along the field boundary. Keep along the field boundary beside the paddocks and once at the far corner the path crosses the boundary and turns left along the field edge and up to the road. Turn right and follow the road back to the staithe.

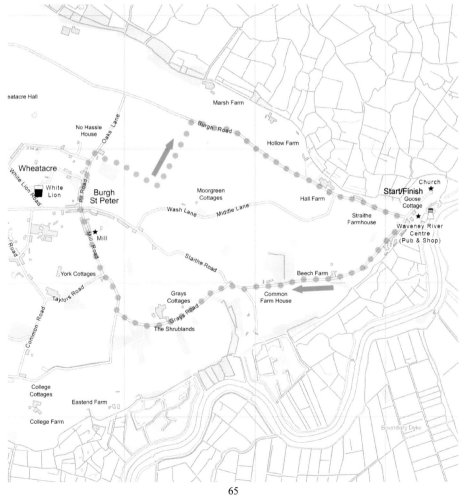

65

The Mill, Burgh St Peter

Burgh St Peter Mill was originally 5 storeys high but the top two were removed in the 1950s. The mill now stands at just three storeys with no cap or sails and converted into a dwelling.

Cantley

River Yare

Cantley

Cantley is a small village along the northern banks of the River Yare close to Reedham and Brundall overshadowed by the massive complex that is Cantley Sugar Factory. The village has the Reedcutter Arms by the staithe but no other amenities, with the closest being in Reedham or Strumpshaw. The village has its own train station which links to nearby villages as well as Norwich and Great Yarmouth. Cantley Marshes forms part of a large 672 acre nature reserve along the River Yare with a series of footpaths exploring the area.

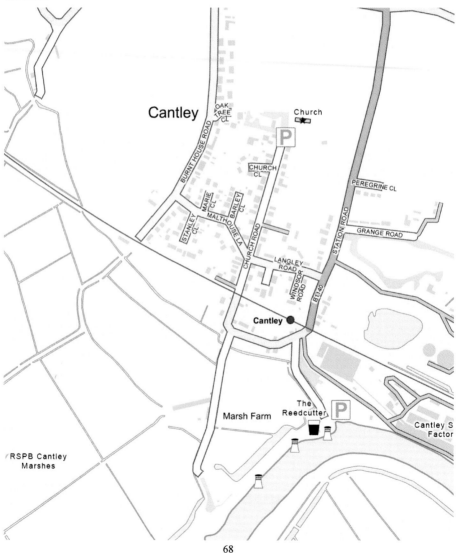

RSPB Cantley Marshes

RSPB Cantley Marshes sits alongside the River Yare and the village of Cantley and is home to some rare insects and bird species. Numerous public footpaths explore the marshes and riverbank habitats so take the binoculars and camera to see what you can find.

RSPB Cantley Marshes

From Cantley Staithe, follow the riverbank footpath in front of the Reedcutters pub and past a section of mooring. After a short distance the path splits by a sewage works, here keep left along the riverbank path and follow it close to the River Yare as it gently begins to bend round to the right and another split in the path. Turn right and follow the path through part of RSPB Cantley Marshes to the north east. The path is fairly straight as it makes its way back to Cantley and shortly before arriving at the village the path bends to the left and then to the right and up to the railway line. Cross the line safely and onto Burnt House Road opposite and then turn right down Malthouse Lane. At the crossroads ahead continue straight onto Langley Road and at the junction turn right onto Station Road which leads up to a railway crossing. Cross safely and bear right then take the first left signposted to Cantley Staithe. Continue back to the staithe at the end of the road.

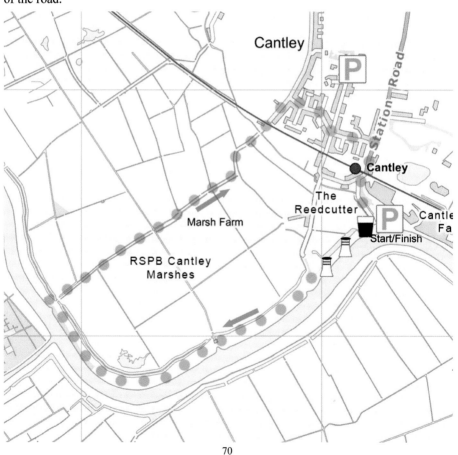

Geese at Cantley Marshes

Walk 16:	**Distance:** 5.9km (3.7 Miles)
River Yare Linear	**Time:** 2 Hours
	Parking: Church Car Park **NR13 3SN**

This is a linear walk so use of public transport to arrive back at the start is required. Prior research into train times is required from Buckenham Station to Cantley Station.

From Cantley Staithe follow the riverbank path in front of the Reedcutter Pub and past a section of moorings. The path splits just past a sewage works where you need to keep left close to the riverbank. The path sticks close to the River Yare as it gently bends round to the right and shortly ahead you may notice another split. Keep left again, sticking close to the River Yare as it meanders gently to the north west. Cross the bridge over Fleet Dike and up to Buckenham Ferry Drainage Mill where it continues further along a trackway that becomes more well defined the closer you get to RSPB Buckenham Marshes. The path branches off the track up onto the riverbank just before reaching the RSPB Reserve and then heads down to the car park and bird hide. After enjoying the view from the bird hide follow the access track north east up to the railway line and Buckenham Station. Use the train service to get back to Cantley.

Hardley Mill and the River Yare

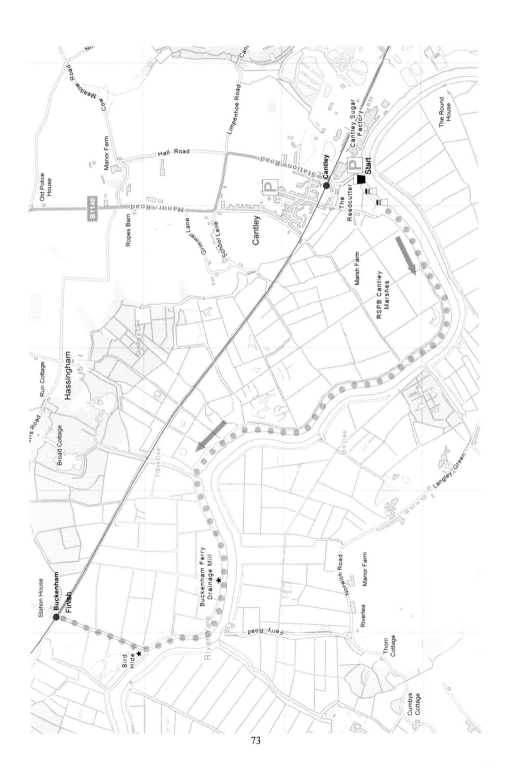

73

Walk 17:
Cantley Church

Distance: 2.4km (1.5 Miles)
Time: 1 Hour
Parking: Church Car Park   **NR13 3SN**

From Cantley Staithe follow the road away from the river and up to the train station. Cross the railway line safely and follow Station Road north out of the village using the pavement to keep off the road. Cross the road onto the left pavement and follow this until it ends at a public footpath on the left. Continue along this footpath to the church of St Margaret, turning left into the church yard and onto Church Road. Head south along Church Road in a straight line to a crossing over the railway line where you need to cross safely and continue along the lane on the other side. At the fork just ahead bear right heading south along a track past Marsh Farm and a small sewage works up onto the riverbank path. Turn left and follow the riverbank path past some moorings and to The Reedcutter pub by the staithe.

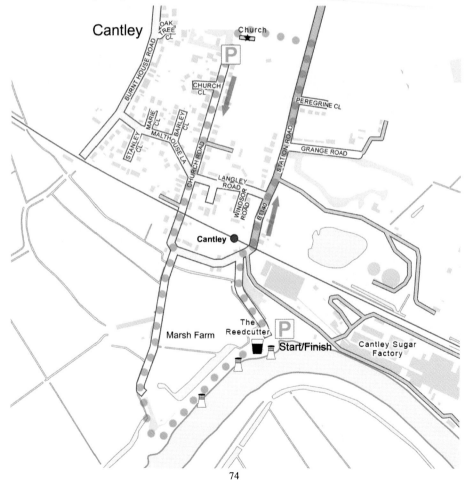

Church of St Margaret, Cantley

The beautiful church of St Margaret in Cantley likely dates to the 15th Century or earlier and was largely restored in 1867. The church is built from flint with stone dressings and given a Grade II* listing.

Claxton

River Yare

Claxton

Claxton is a tiny village between Rockland St Mary and Loddon. The Beauchamp Arms is located on the edge of the village along the River Yare and is the closest place to moor up and explore this part of the Broads. There are no other facilities in the village with the closest shops being in Loddon a few miles down the road, but it is worth taking a leisurely stroll around the village as the remains of Claxton Castle can be seen from the road and the church is set back in a remote countryside location.

St Andrew's Church, Claxton

The Grade I listed church of St Andrew in Claxton is set back from the main village. The building dates to the 12th Century and it is thought the original Saxon settlement of Claxton began in this area and moved down towards the marshes in the middle ages.

Claxton Castle

Claxton Castle was originally a manor house that was granted permission to be fortified in 1340. The Grade II* remains form part of a scheduled ancient monument that incorporate earthworks and other surviving remnants of the fortification which was largely demolished 17th Century to make way for Claxton Hall alongside.

This walk can also be completed from Rockland St Mary staithe providing parking and free mooring.

From the Beauchamp Arms moorings, follow the riverbank west past the pub, keeping the River Yare on the right. Stick to the riverbank path as it completes a gentle arc around Claxton Marshes and after 1.5km the path turns left, away from the River Yare and along Short Dike. The path passes an RSPB Hide which overlooks Rockland Broad and follows the edge of the marsh to Rockland Staithe. Once at the staithe continue to the road and turn left. The road is followed south to Claxton Corner and bends round to the left with views towards Claxton Castle (the castle is on private land so please keep to the road). 800m past the castle there is a public bridleway on the left which first follows Mill Lane and then turns into a track and follows a path through narrow fields with dykes on both sides. The path eventually arrives at the River Yare with the Beauchamp Arms just to the right.

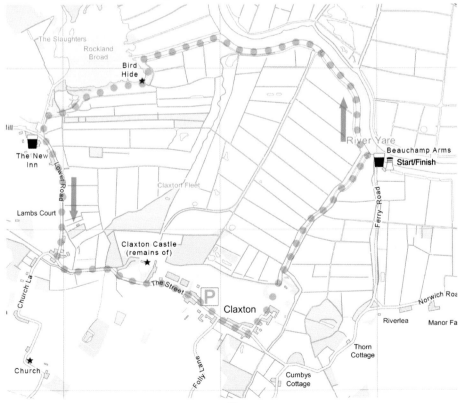

Claxton Marshes

Geldeston

River Waveney

Geldeston

Geldeston is a small village just west of Beccles and at the limit of navigation for watercraft. The Locks Inn is located by the River Waveney on the south side of the village along with the free moorings and parking, and The Wherry Inn is located in the village centre. Rowan Craft is the local boatyard offering motorboat and canoe hire to explore the southern broads and also has a caravan and camping site.

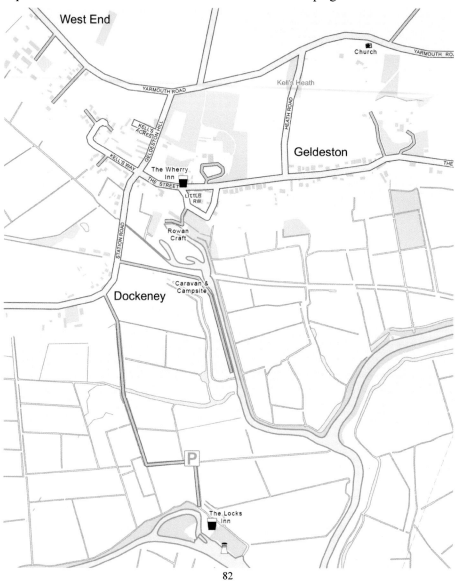

St Michael's Church, Geldeston

The Grade II* listed church of St Michael in Geldeston was remodelled in the 19th Century but originally dates as far back as the 12th Century. It is one of only 124 round tower churches in Norfolk.

From the free mooring close to the Locks Inn follow the path alongside the pub and onto the track. Follow the track past the parking area and continue to the road. Turn right and follow the lane up to the crossroads and turn right along The Street. Turn right down the lane opposite the Wherry Inn and turn right again along the right of way around the left hand side of Rowan Craft. The path passes through the trees and along the river towards the Waveney past vast open grazing marsh and once at the River Waveney the path turns left and begins to follow it north east. A boathouse is passed and the path gently curves round to the right for 650m where there the path turns away from the river and splits with the option to continue ahead or to the right. Take the path straight ahead away from the river which leads to the road and turn left following it to the junction. After 350m just after Geldeston Lodge is a track called Snakes Lane. Take this track north and bear right until the track arrives at the road. Turn left past the parish church and take the first lane on the left (Heath Road). After 150m take the bridleway on the right which leads in a straight line to the road and continue left. Take the first road on the left (Geldeston Hill) and continue ahead at the crossroads looking out for Locks Lane on the left which will lead back to the car park and eventually to the moorings.

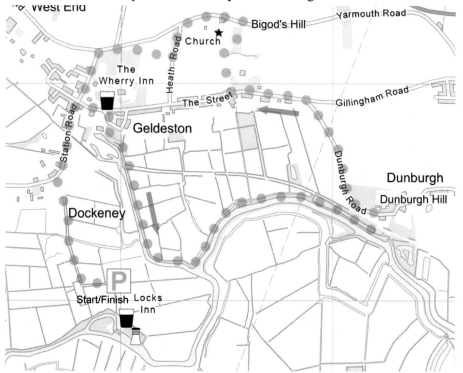

River Waveney

Langley

River Yare

Langley

Langley is a tiny village along the River Yare close to Loddon. The village has no facilities or amenities but does offer free mooring along Langley dyke and a restaurant at Langley Abbey Estate which used to be a museum but now mainly caters for weddings. Hints of the ruins can be seen from the road side and access lane to Langley Dike but sadly there is no public access to the ruins themselves. Additional parking is available at the end of the track to Langley Dike.

Langley Staithe

Langley Abbey

Langley Abbey was founded by Robert fitzRoger in 1195 and historically was open to the public as a museum but now sadly closed and only used as a wedding venue. Its beautiful ruins have been incorporated into some of the more modern buildings and protected as a scheduled ancient monument and Grade I listed building.

From Langley Staithe follow the access track to the road and turn right. Follow the road past Langley Abbey and into Langley Green. After approximately 1.2km the road leaves Langley Green and there is a public footpath on the left across open fields. Take this path as it heads south across the field and up to a boundary and continue a further 350m up to a small clump of trees. The path turns left here across the field in a diagonal line to the far eastern corner and onto a track. Turn left along the track which heads up to the road and turn right. The road then passes Langley Abbey again and up to the access track to the moorings.

Langley Staithe

Loddon

River Chet

Loddon

Loddon is a small market town at the end of the River Chet and borders the neighbouring village of Chedgrave. The staithe provides free mooring and a car park for visitors and the perfect place to set off exploring the local area. There are several pubs and shops in the town centre including The Swan, The Kings Head, and The Angel, with the White Horse in neighbouring Chedgrave. There are shops and convenience stores along the high street as well as numerous takeaways to suit most tastes. Boat hire is available from the nearby boatyard allowing exploration of the River Chet and Yare.

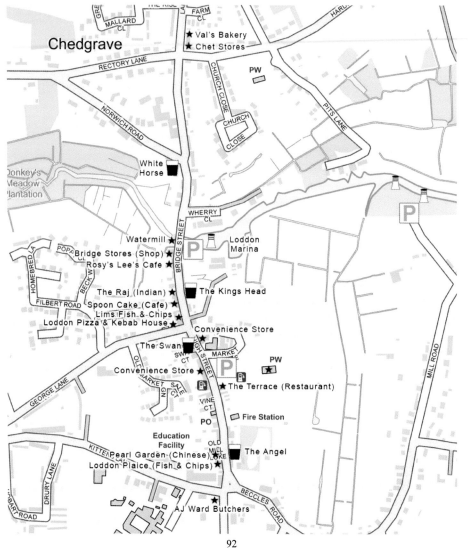

Holy Trinity Church, Loddon

The Holy Trinity Church in Loddon was built around 1490 and sits alongside the Wherryman's Way, a 37 mile long distance path from Great Yarmouth to Norwich following the River Yare. The church has been given a Grade I listing.

Walk 21:	Distance: 2.1km (1.3 Miles)
River Chet	Time: 1 Hour
	Parking: Staithe Car Park **NR14 6EZ**

From the staithe and car park, head to the road and turn left. Just after the Kings Head pub there is a small road/track marked as a Public Footpath towards Loddon Marina. Follow the footpath past the boatyard and along the riverbank of the Chet. This is a lovely section of the walk with wildlife and wild flowers in abundance. After 300m there is a footbridge over a dyke and then the path meanders through a small section of woodland. Keep to the left and follow the riverbank until you can see a car park on the right. Cross the car park and follow the country lane for about 150m and turn right. Follow this lane for 170m keeping an eye out for the public footpath on the right (directly opposite another footpath on the left). Follow this footpath (not to be mistaken for the driveway directly next to it) towards the grand Holy Trinity Church. On arrival at the Church head towards The Swan Inn along the High Street and turn right. Follow the high street all the way back to the staithe.

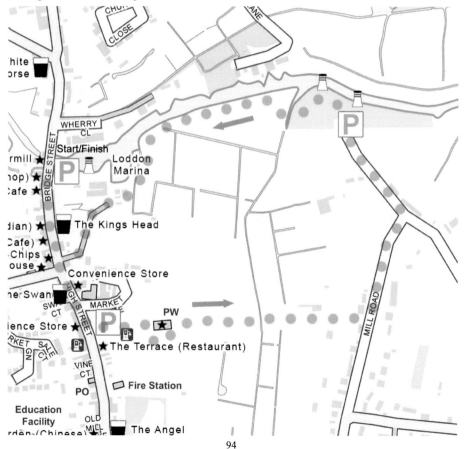

Loddon Water Mill

Loddon Watermill was built in the 18th Century but a mill has been recorded in Loddon since the Domesday Book was written. The mill was almost destroyed in 1912 when the surrounding area was flooded due to torrential rain. (Image on Page 91).

Loddon Staithe

Walk 22:	**Distance:** 8.2km (5.1 Miles)
Hardley Flood	**Time:** 2 Hours 30 Minutes
	Parking: Staithe Car Park **NR14 6EZ**

From Loddon Staithe head up to the road and turn right, heading north towards Chedgrave. At the bend turn right down Langley Road and at the crossroads just ahead turn right along Hardley Road with Chedgrave Church just on the right behind the trees in about 80m. Just past the church turn right down Pits Lane and follow it to the end of the road where it arrives at the River Chet. Bear left up onto the riverbank path along the Chet heading east for 1.2km where the path arrives at the edge of Hardley Flood. The path meanders along the edge of Hardley Flood for 1.2km where it then leaves the Broad and continues along the riverbank a further 900m to a track heading off to the left. Follow this track heading west to the entrance driveway for Hardley Hall. Cross the driveway onto the track opposite where it heads west and eventually arrives at the road. Turn left and follow Lower Hardley Road for 1.5km back into the village of Chedgrave and at the crossroads turn left back into Loddon.

Note that the path along Hardley Flood is currently closed. Funding has been found to rebuild the path which is due to be complete around 2024/5.

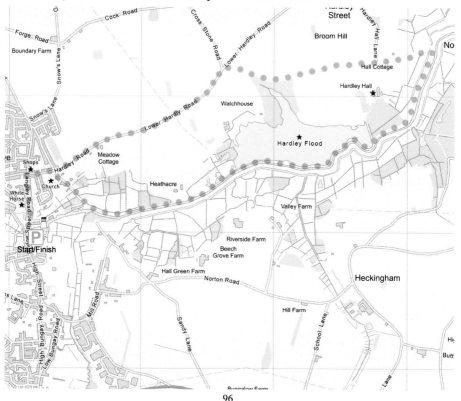

96

Hardley Flood

Hardley Flood is a 123 acre nature reserve and site of special scientific interest (SSSI). The area provides an overspill for the River Chet which runs alongside and is home to many species of birds and insects.

Hardley Hall

Hardley Hall is a stunning Grade II* listed Elizabethan House dating back to the mid or late 16th Century. Although the path doesn't pass too close to the house it can be seen along parts of the walk.

Norwich

River Wensum

Norwich

Norwich is the principal city of Norfolk with the far western edge of the National Park, just within its boundary. The cities history dates back thousands of years with the Romans building Venta Icenorum just to the south of present day Norwich. During Saxon times the city moved north to its current location where it was fortified after the Norman invasion. A large castle was built in the centre, complete with city walls and a bustling trade made this the second largest city in England after London. During this time one of the most spectacular and tallest cathedrals was built, second only to Salisbury. The present day spire stands at a height of 96m (315ft) and home to a nesting pair of Peregrine Falcons. There are dozens of historic buildings around the city including St Andrews Hall, Strangers Hall and Dragon Hall as well as the medieval cobbled streets of Elm Hill and Tombland. Norwich is also the perfect city to do some shopping, with countless chain and independent shops set up around the castle, two shopping malls and the largest undercover outdoor market in the country. On the outskirts of the city sits Whitlingham Country Park and cafe, with several miles of wheelchair friendly paths around the wildlife rich habitats of the River Yare and Whitlingham Lake.

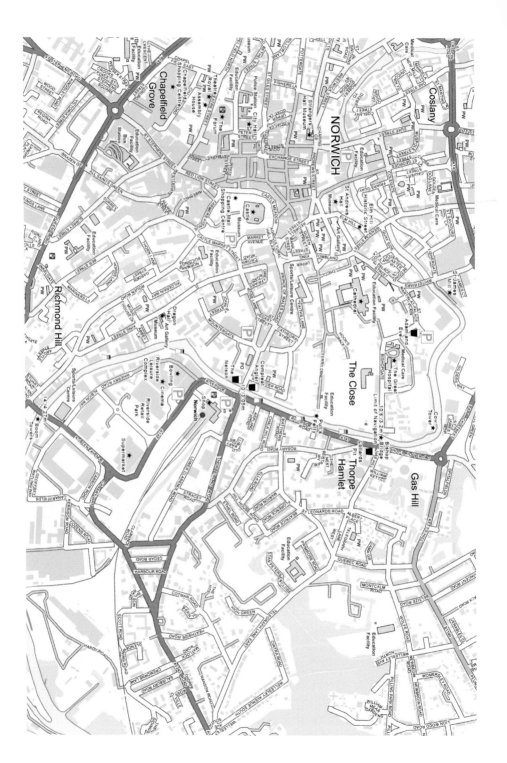

Norwich Castle

Norwich Castle is a spectacular Grade I listed building that was constructed in 1067, just one year after the Norman Conquest and sits high on an artificial mound known as a Motte. Throughout the years it has been used as a prison and is now open as a museum detailing the history of Norwich and displaying archaeological finds discovered during the excavation of Castle Mall shopping centre and those found locally. There are guided tours down into the dungeons as well as to the battlements allowing for some amazing views over the city.

City Walls

Norwich City Walls are extensive and surrounded the medieval city, with no buildings being constructed outside of this boundary until after 1779. The walls were built between 1294-1343 with several towers remaining to this day including the impressive Cow Tower, Black Tower and Boom Towers. The remains are protected as a scheduled ancient monument.

Elm Hill

Elm Hill is a superbly preserved medieval cobbled street in the city centre. The surrounding buildings along the street mostly date to the Tudor period and have been used in several film and television productions.

Norwich Cathedral

The construction of Norwich Cathedral started in 1096 and has gone through several phases of reconstruction and repair. At 96m tall it is the second tallest cathedral in the country, with only Salisbury Cathedral being slightly higher. The Cathedral also has the second largest cloisters in England, again second only to Sailisbury and protected as a Grade I listed building.

St Andrew's Hall

The construction of Norwich Cathedral started in 1096 and has gone through several phases of reconstruction and repair. At 96m tall it is the second tallest cathedral in the country, with only Salisbury Cathedral being slightly higher. The Cathedral also has the second largest cloisters in England, again second only to Sailisbury and protected as a Grade I listed building.

Norwich Guildhall

The construction of Norwich Cathedral started in 1096 and has gone through several phases of reconstruction and repair. At 96m tall it is the second tallest cathedral in the country, with only Salisbury Cathedral being slightly higher. The Cathedral also has the second largest cloisters in England, again second only to Sailisbury and protected as a Grade I listed building.

Assembly House

The complex history of the Assembly House begins back in 1248 when a Chapel and Hospice were founded on the site and later converted into a College for Secular Priests in 1278. The college fell into disuse around the time of the dissolution of the monasteries and many of the buildings were demolished. In 1754 the present house was built and incorporated some of the remaining features of the college including the 15th Century brick undercroft.

City Hall

The Art Deco building that is Norwich City Hall was completed in 1938 to the highest standards available at the time; even the bricks were made specially for the hall. City Hall overlooks the bustling market below and has been protected with a Grade II* listing.

Pulls Ferry

Pulls Ferry is a wonderfully preserved watergate which was used to transport goods from the river into the city. The Grade II* flint building dates to the 15th Century and underwent restorations in 1948-9.

Bishop Bridge

Bishop Bridge is a lovely Grade II* listed building dating as far back as 1340. It is built of flint and brick spanning three arches over the River Wensum and is a scheduled ancient monument.

Cow Tower

The Cow Tower on the shores of the River Wensum is one of the earliest purpose built artillery blockhouses in England. Construction commenced in 1398-9 away from the main city walls to give it a strategic advantage in defending the cities north eastern side which is flanked by higher ground. To combat this higher ground the tower soared to over 50ft and armed with numerous types of cannon. The structure is protected as a scheduled ancient monument.

St James' Mill

St James Mill overlooks the gentle flowing waters of the River Wensum but was once a bustling noisy yarn mill. The Grade I listed building dates to 1839 and built on the site of the Whitefriars who worshiped at a friary here in the 13th Century of which a single arch and an undercroft remain.

The Great Hospital

St Giles Hospital, referred to as The Great Hospital was founded in 1249 on a site just north west of the present day Cathedral, close to the River Wensum. The hospital is rare because of the continued use through history with many of the medieval buildings remainging as part of the hospital. All of the original buildings associated with the hospital are protected as Grade I, with other parts listed as Grade II.

Strangers Hall
Strangers Hall, now a museum, was once a series of shops and houses dating back to the 14th Century. Open throughout the year, the museum is well worth visiting and experiencing its complex history.

Dragon Hall
Dragon Hall is a stunning example of a 14th Century merchants house and is currently home to the National Centre for Writing. The building is thought to be completely unique in Europe and has tours available on set days throughout the year.

Walk 23:	**Distance:** 7.5km (4.7 Miles)
Historic Norwich	**Time:** 3 Hours
	Parking: Riverside Car Park **NR1 1XA**

From Norwich Yacht Station head along the river to the bridge by the Compleat Angler and The Nelson. Turn right in front of the Compleat Angler signposted as the Riverside Walk and follow the path up to Pull's Ferry. Bear right past Pull's Ferry back along the riverbank path and follow the riverside walk north to the road by Bishop Bridge. Continue straight ahead along Cotman Fields road signposted to the Cow Tower where the path rejoins the riverbank and curves round to the Cow Tower just ahead. Follow the riverbank path west past the footbridge and round a sharp bend in the river with St James' Mill opposite. Continue to the bridge and turn left past the church and take

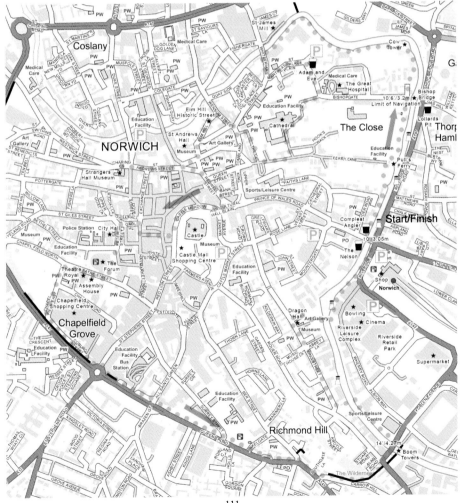

the first left along St Martin At Palace Plain with one of the Cathedral Gates to the right. Follow the road round the sharp bend to the right near the Adam and Eve Pub and at the next sharp bend left marks the location of the Great Hospital. Turn to face the Cathedral and follow the path along the wall towards it which passes around the eastern end of this breathtaking structure. Continue past the car park and turn right towards The Ethelbert Gate, turning right just before it towards the main entrance for the Cathedral. Turn left through the Erpingham Gate onto the main road and cross to the other side. Turn right and bear left along Wensum Street looking out for Elm Hill on the left just after the church. Follow Elm Hill cobbled street and at the sharp bend just past the church turn right which leads in front of St Andrews Hall and progresses up to St Andrews Street. Turn right along St Andrews Street for just over 150m to Strangers Hall and once seen backtrack along St Andrews Street and follow it past St Andrews Hall and round to the right along Bank Plain and towards the Anglia Television Building. Follow the pavement round to the right and around the bus station area known as Castle Meadow with the Castle Keep up to the left. Turn right along Davey Place which is signposted to Norwich Market and once at the market turn right towards the Medieval Guildhall just ahead to the left. Follow Gaol Hill up to City Hall and turn left following the pavement in front of the building and up to the Forum. Continue past the Forum to the road and turn right past The Assembly House and Theatre Royal and up to Chapelfield Gardens. Head into the gardens and follow the path past the gazebo and bear left along the path towards the car entrance to Chapel Field Shopping Centre. Follow the road along the apartments keeping the old City Wall on the right with evidence of several towers on

River Wensum

The Forum

this side. The path arrives at a roundabout with an underpass, head into the underpass and turn left leading up to the City Wall again with evidence of another tower. Follow the main road (Queens Road) for 600m, past Finkelgate and up to Ber Street. On the left by the entrance to Ber Street is evidence of a large tower along the line of the City Wall. Continue past Ber Street looking out for Carrow Hill on the left just ahead. After just a few metres there is a path on the left which joins the City Wall once again and passes several amazing towers as it descends down to the road. Ahead to the left is Carrow Road Bridge, cross the bridge and turn right down to the riverbank by the Boom Towers and then right again heading under the bridge keeping the river on the left. Follow the riverbank for a short way to the next footbridge and cross over to the other side. Turn right along King Street and after about 350m Dragon Hall is just on the right. Turn right just after Dragon Hall to cross the River Wensum again and then turn left along the riverbank which eventually arrive back at Norwich Yacht Station.

Walk 24: Whitlingham Broad	Distance: 3.7km (2.3 Miles) Time: 1 Hour 30 Minutes Parking: Whitlingham Park NR14 8TR

From Whitlingham Country Park Cafe, follow the path over to the lakeshore and turn right. A path hugs the shore running parallel to the country lane just over to the right. The path continues to the far side of the Broad where there is an option to either follow the edge of Whitlingham Broad or instead follow the banks of the River Yare, both of which merge just the other side of the woods. The circular path follows a narrow strip of land between the River Yare and Whitlingham Broad with a short detour on the left leading down to a lookout over the broad. Return to the main path and turn left following the track round to the Whitlingham Adventure Centre just past the mooring area. Follow the path round to the left between the two broads and bear left again. Just in the trees on the right are the ruins of Trowse Newton Hall and just beyond is the main visitor centre and cafe.

Whitlingham Lake

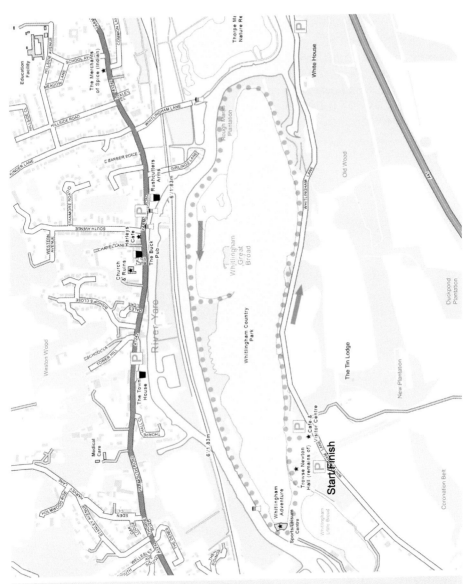

Whitlingham Country Park

Whitlingham Country Park is a beautiful area on the edge of Norwich and incorporates two Broads, marsh, river and woodland habitats. The park is the perfect place to enjoy spotting the local wildlife from the 2 mile long wheelchair friendly trail around Whitlingham Great Broad. Why not taste the delightful food in the cafe before setting out to explore the ruins of Trowse Newton Hall or delving deeper into the prehistoric history of the area.

Trowse Newton Hall

The interesting ruins of Trowse Newton Hall in Whitlingham Country Park date back to the mid 15th Century and once was the proud home of the Priors of Norwich. Later, after the dissolution of the monasteries it became home to the Deans followed by a farm house and eventually demolished in 1860. The ruins are now protected as a Grade II listed building and can be leisurely explored on the walk around the country park.

| Walk 25: **Thorpe Marshes** | **Distance:** 3.0km (1.9 Miles)
 Time: 1 Hour 30 Minutes
 Parking: Roadside Layby   **NR7 0HF** |

From the mooring at Thorpe St Andrew, head up to the road and turn right. Follow the road past the Rushcutters Arms and continue up to a narrow lane on the right called Whitlingham Lane. Head down Whitlingham Lane, over the railway line and up to the river. The footpath passes a small area of mooring and along the riverbank with Thorpe Marshes over to the left. The riverbank path heads south and then bends round to the left with plenty of opportunities to stop and look over the marshes and open water. Shortly the path turns away from the river and up to the marsh where the path splits. Keep left along the edge of the marsh and open water on the left. The path heads north through the marshes and bends to the left leading back to the track close to the moorings you were at earlier. Turn right along Whitlingham Lane, back over the railway and up to the main road, with the moorings and parking area just down the road to the left.

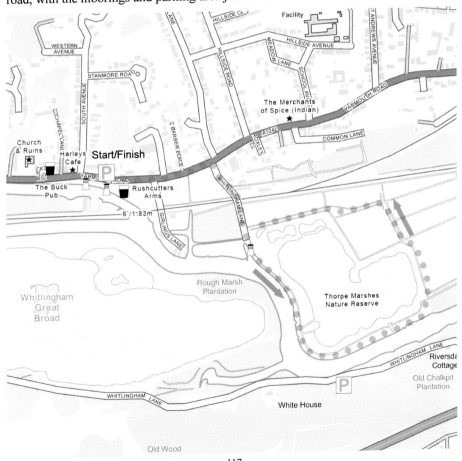

Thorpe Marshes

Thorpe Marshes is a superb small nature reserve owned and managed by Norfolk Wildlife Trust and includes nature trails around a small wetland scrape, along the riverbank and through the marshes. The reserve is home to grass snakes, the elusive and rare water vole and numerous species of dragonfly.

Oulton Broad

Oulton Dyke

Oulton Broad

Oulton Broad sits just to the west of Lowestoft and links to the sea by Mutford Lock. The large open broad is bordered by the lovely Nicholas Everitt Park with plenty of moorings and large car park for visitors. The park is home to Lowestoft Museum inside a lovely Grade II listed house dating to the late 18th Century. There are plenty of local shops, restaurants and takeaways to enjoy with more just a few minutes walk from the yacht station along the high street. Oulton Broad has two train stations on different lines, one linking to Norwich via Reedham and the other bound for Beccles and eventually onto London. The Angles Way long distance path passes right through Oulton Broad which can be enjoyed by more adventurous walkers and use public transport to return to the village (a part of this route is completed as a walk from Somerleyton). The broad plays host to plenty of watersports also, including powerboat racing and day boat hire.

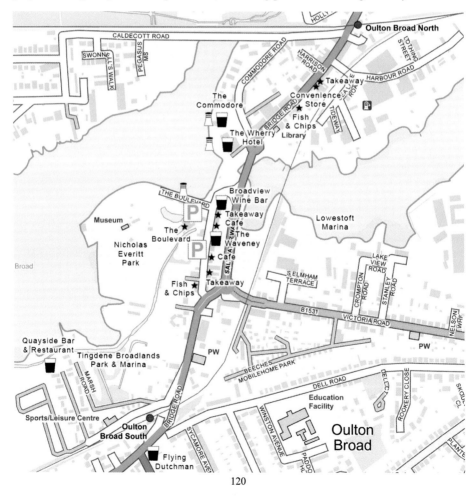

Carlton Marshes

Carlton Marshes is a beautiful nature reserve owned and managed by Suffolk Wildlife Trust. A recent grant of over £4million has allowed the trust to begin work on building a new visitor centre and enlarge the specially protected wetland to encourage a wider range of species. Birds such as Marsh Harrier, Bearded Tit, Cetti's Warbler and Barn Owls are frequently seen flying over the marshes so don't forget the camera and binoculars.

From Oulton Broad Yacht Station, head out of the car park and turn right along Bridge Road and as the road joins the A1117 keep right heading south past a small car park. Bear right along Marsh Road just past the car park and at the split just after the bend in the road keep right. At the next sharp bend there is a footpath off to the left along a hedgeline followed by marsh and then over the access road to the Crooked Barn Restaurant. Continue along the field edge and at the next field the path turns right and proceeds up to a split at a track. Keep right and follow the path up to the reedbed just ahead then turn left following the flood defence wall through Carlton Marshes Nature Reserve. The path heads in a fairly straight line to the west and then bends round to the right along another straight path followed by curves around the marshes. After another straight section of path the route heads down onto a track, turn left here and follow the track south east to the visitor centre and car park for the Suffolk Wildlife Trust. Follow the Angles Way on the left just before the car park which takes a gentle bend to the right and up to a sharp bend where you were at earlier. Turn right here heading along the fence and turn left to the drive for the Crooked Barn and backtrack along the path past the marsh and onto Marsh Road. Continue ahead and then once close to the road bridge follow the road round to the left following it north back to Oulton Broad.

Nicholas Everitt Park

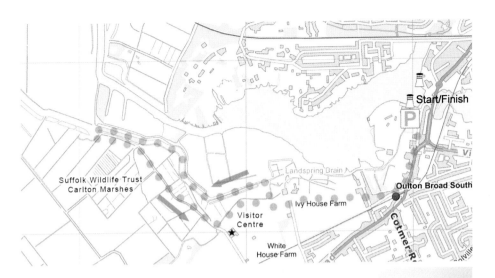

Start/Finish

P

Suffolk Wildlife Trust
Carlton Marshes

Landspring Drain

Oulton Broad South

Ivy House Farm

Visitor
Centre

Cotmer Rd

White
House Farm

Carlton Marshes

Postwick

River Yare

Postwick (pronounced Poz-ick) is a tiny village on the edge of Norwich. It has a small staithe with enough parking for a few cars and mooring for a couple of boats. At one point there used to be a ferry crossing the River Yare over to Surlingham which ceased in 1939 due to a collision on the water. There are no shops or pubs in the village, with just a hundred or so houses built around the central parish church. About 1.5 miles from the staithe is the Postwick Park & Ride service into Norwich City Centre allowing for access into the city from this side.

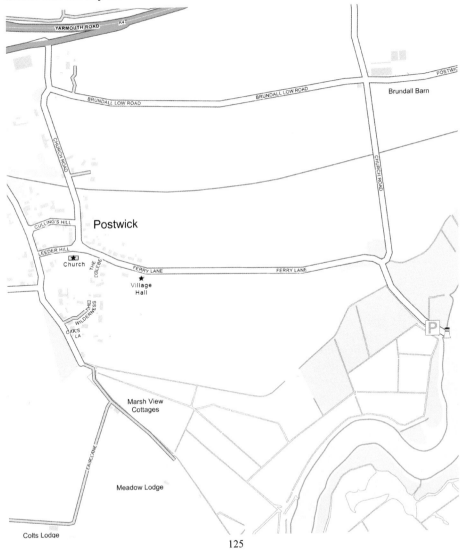

From Postwick Staithe follow the access track back to the road and then turn left. Follow Ferry Lane in a relatively straight line west into the village of Postwick, passing the Village Hall and Social Club first and then up to a split in the road. This split marks the entrance to All Saints Church just on the left. Leave the church yard and turn left along Leeder Hill and at the junction turn left again. Follow Oaks Lane for 250m to a turn on the left called The Wilderness. A public footpath follows the narrow lane to the end where it turns right down an alley to the field and then turns left up to the road. Turn right and follow the road up to the access track for Postwick Staithe and turn right, following the track back to the river.

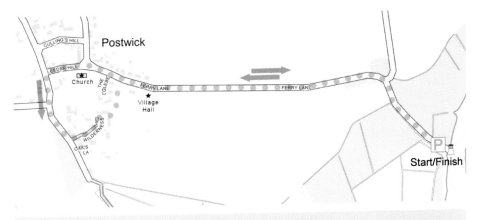

All Saints Church, Postwick

The beautiful Grade II* listed church of All Saints sits in the centre of Postwick dates to the late 13th Century with a 14th Century two-stage west tower.

Reedham

River Yare

Reedham

Reedham is a small village along the River Yare between Norwich and Great Yarmouth. It has three pubs, the Lord Nelson just by the staithe, the Ferry Inn slightly further down river and the Ship just by the railway viaduct. The village has some facilities including a Post Office, a small food store and electric hookup by the staithe. Reedham Ferry is quite a famous place on the southern broads as it is the only crossing of the river between Norwich and Great Yarmouth and can take around two cars across at a time. The local train station is within walking distance from the free parking and moorings, with the choice of going to Great Yarmouth, Norwich or Lowestoft. Just a short walk down the road takes you to Pettitts Animal Adventure Park which is great for young children and families. It is open every day during the season and has lots of rides and attractions and plenty of animals to see. Although not shown on the map, Reedham Chain Ferry and pub are just quarter of a mile to the west.

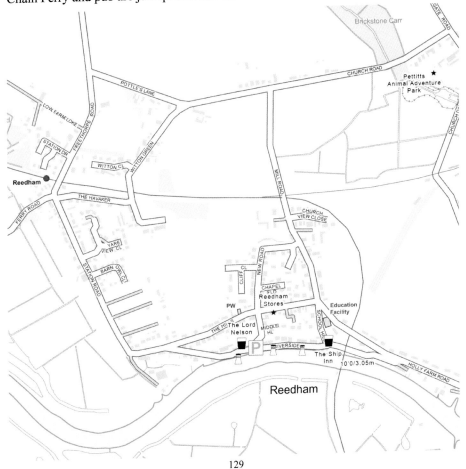

St John the Baptist, Reedham

Reedham Church is located a short walk from the village centre and moorings, but is worth a visit for its solitude. The tower was built in 1447, but the church suffered great damage in a fire in 1981. It has since been restored and given a Grade I listing.

This is a linear walk from Reedham to Cantley so it is vital to check train times prior to setting out to ensure safe arrival back in Reedham.

From the staithe parking and mooring turn left along the road and follow it to the west up to a junction. Turn left and then round the sharp right hand bend and at the end of the road you will be near the Train Station. At the junction turn left along Ferry Road and follow it until you reach Reedham Ferry and the Ferry Inn. Briefly head past the Ferry Inn, looking for some steps up onto the riverbank on the right just by the river. Once on the riverbank path stick to this as it meanders its way towards Cantley. There are several paths leading off into the fields but ignore these, you want to stick to the riverbank path as close as possible (except for two sections where the path skirts round a large overspill pool - originally the public right of way was on the river side but this has become too dangerous). The path passes the isolated tower of Limpenhoe Drainage Mill and on the opposite bank the superbly preserved Hardley Drainage Mill. As you begin to approach Cantley the path arrives at a track and splits, keep left here close to the riverbank and follow the path between the Sugar Factory and the River Yare. At the other side of the factory the path arrives at Cantley Staithe where you need to turn right along the access road and once at the end the train station will be directly in front.

Reedham Ferry

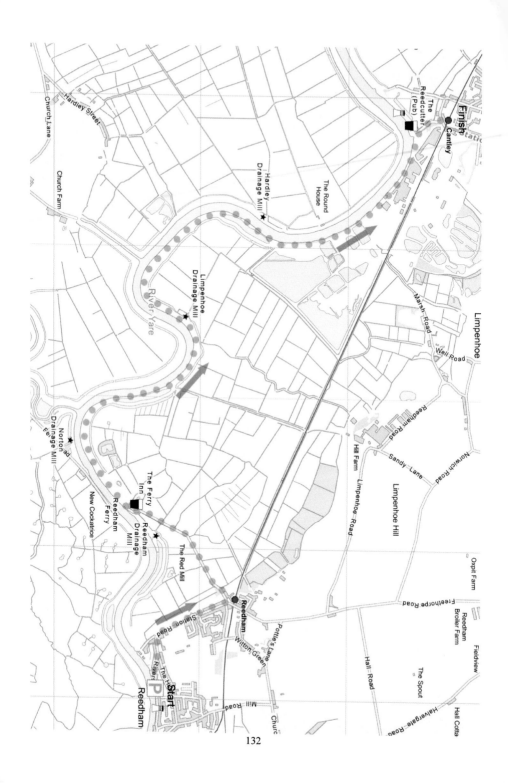

Rockland St Mary

River Yare

Rockland St Mary is a small village along the River Yare with a history dating back to Anglo Saxon times. The village is set out over a long street with the staithe and free mooring on the far eastern side and parish church on the western end. The New Inn is located opposite the staithe and in the village centre is a small post office and convenience store. Alongside the staithe is a large free car park for visitors who plan on exploring the village or one of the local nature reserves. Just to the east is RSPB Rockland Broad Nature Reserve with a bird hide overlooking the broad which is home to plenty of wildlife. About a mile to the north is the Ted Ellis Nature Reserve, with numerous trails around marsh and woodland exploring this wonderful area.

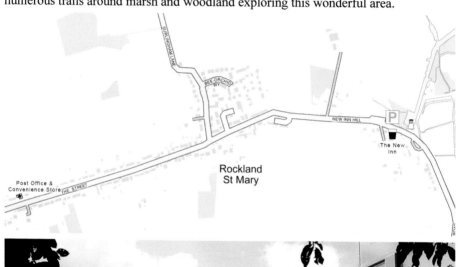

RSPB Rockland Broad

Rockland Marshes are owned and managed by the RSPB who have also placed a bird hide overlooking the reedbed and broad. The area links in with the surrounding nature reserves creating an unbr ken line of protected wetlands along the Yare Valley. There's a chance to see Reed Warblers, Kingfishers, Marsh Harriers and Great Crested Grebes from the hide so take binoculars and a camera with you!

Walk 29:
Rockland Broad

Distance: 1.8km (1.1 Miles)
Time: 1 Hour
Parking: Staithe Car Park　　**NR14 7HP**

From Rockland Staithe follow the lane alongside the moorings (signposted as the Wherryman's Way) where it bends to the right. Keep left along the flood defence wall beside the marsh for approximately 800m where you will come across a bird hide just on the left which overlooks Rockland Broad. Just beyond the hide is also a superb viewpoint and a bench overlooking Rockland Broad. After enjoying the views and spotting the wildlife backtrack along the same path to arrive back at Rockland Staithe.

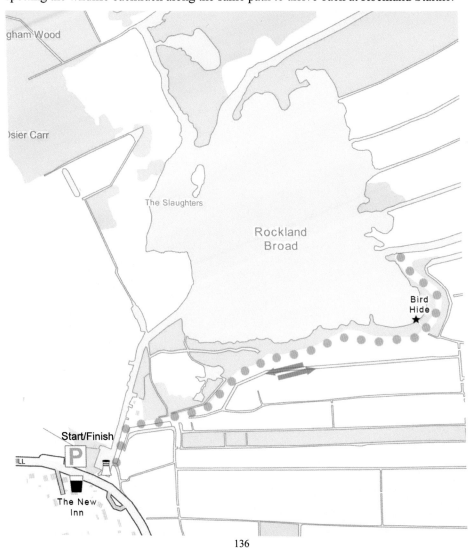

Rockland Marshes

The distance and time above is to the reserve entrance and does not include any of the trails within the reserve so allow extra time for this.

From Rockland Staithe follow the road west for 300m past the car park to a minor road on the right. Turn right along Green Lane which turns into a track through a farm heading north, which then in turn joins a footpath across the field. At the footpath post on the far side of the field turn right towards the woods and follow the path round to the left. Follow this path for 500m to the entrance to the Ted Ellis Nature Reserve just on the right. After following some of the trails around the reserve, retrace your steps back along the fields, through the farm and to the road leading to Rockland Staithe.

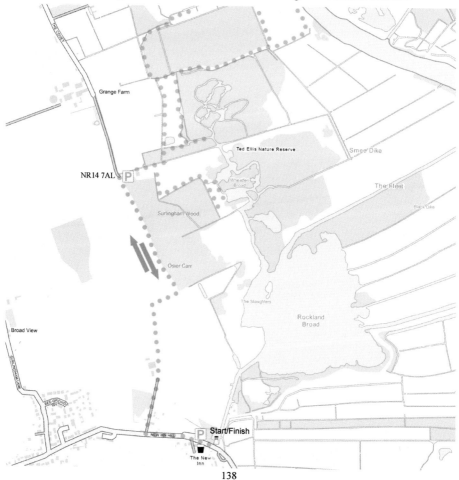

Ted Ellis Nature Reserve

Wheatfen Broad, also known as the Ted Ellis Reserve is a protected area of marsh and wetland sandwiched between Surlingham and Rockland. Ted Ellis (1909 - 1986) was one of the most respected and well known naturalists of his time and documented incredible amounts of detail about the local area around Wheatfen. The Ted Ellis Trust now looks after the reserve along with a group of volunteers and manages the protected habitats and maintains the network of paths through the marshes.

Somerleyton

River Waveney

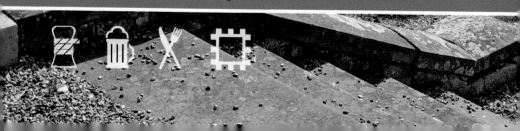

Somerleyton

Somerleyton is a village located along the River Waveney made famous for its spectacular Jacobean style hall which is open to the public. Sadly the village shop and post office have now closed but the Dukes Head pub remains open and near to the public staithe and marina. The village has a small railway station on the Lowestoft to Norwich line which opens up possibilities for some linear walks through the marshes.

Somerleyton Hall

Somerleyton Hall

Somerleyton Hall was built in 1844 but has a small 16th Century core. The Grade II* Listed building is an absolutely stunning Jacobean Style mansion, with vast open parkland to be explored and dozens of rooms to see. The house is open throughout the summer for guided tours and leisurely walks around the estate.

Walk 31: **Herringfleet Mill**	**Distance:** 3.0km (1.9 Miles) **Time:** 1 Hour **Parking:** Staithe Car Park **NR32 5QR**

This is a short linear walk that follows the same path out to Herringfleet Mill and back to Somerleyton Staithe.

From the staithe, face the river and turn right. Follow the path along the moorings and then up onto the riverbank by the Somerleyton Estate signpost. A permissive path along the raised bank heads north west from here, between the reedbeds and in the direction of Herringfleet Mill. A few turns take the path around a small pond and eventually arrives at the stunning Smock Mill. Retrace your steps back to arrive at Somerleyton Staithe.

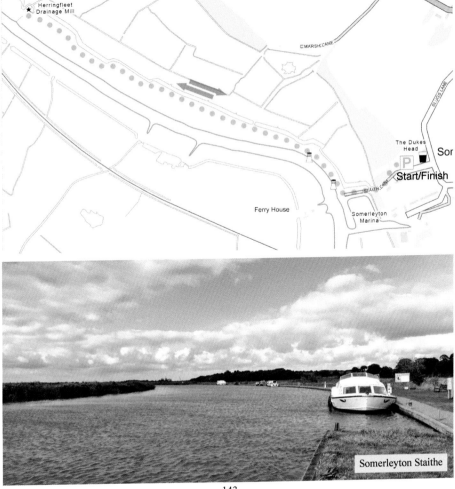

Somerleyton Staithe

Herringfleet Mill

Herringfleet Marsh Mill is a stunning Grade II* listed Smock Mill preserved in full working order. It was constructed in 1820 and remains the last full sized smock mill in the national park.

This walk is a linear route from Somerleyton to Oulton and requires the use of the local train line to return to the start. It is essential to check train times prior to setting out on the route.

From Somerleyton Staithe follow the track away from the river to the road and turn right. At the sharp bend ahead there is a footpath branching off along a track on the right, take this and at the split bear left following the track round towards Somerleyton Marina. This is now the Angles Way and is generally well signposted from here on. The track approaches some buildings just ahead, bear left along the track picking up the path in the far left corner which passes alongside a property and then along the field edge and woodland to the country lane. Turn left and follow Station Road in a straight line to the crossroads and turn left along Waddling Lane. At the split bear left and follow the path round the bend along the edge of woodland to the east. At the next split keep right along Waddling Lane (track) as it gently bends to the left and continues east. Follow the track for 1.5km to another track on the right which almost completes a switchback and leads south west in a straight line between trees and bushes. The track approaches a line of woodland where the path turns left just before it and sticks to the edge of the woodland for a short way. The path then hugs the edge of the woodland until you reach some isolated cottages and the driveway for them.

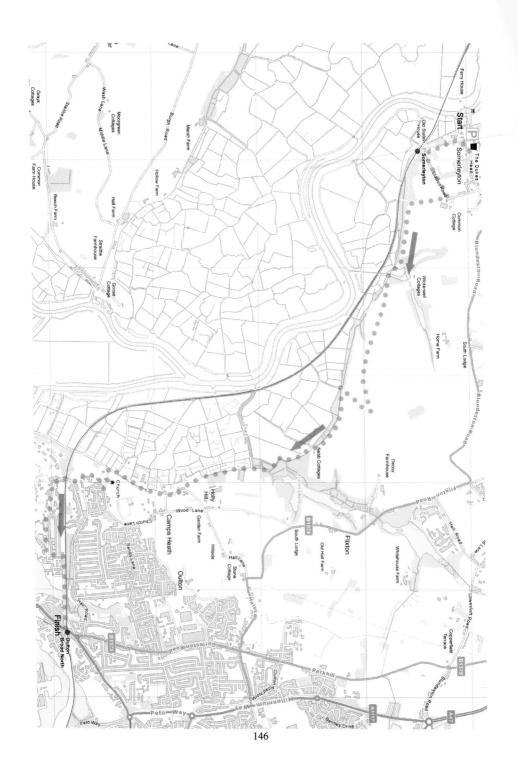

The path bears right then left along the southern edge of the woodland and eventually into the woods along a dyke and out the south side of the woods onto a track by open grazing marsh. Continue south along the track and at the sharp bend the Angles Way continues along the edge of the marsh just to the right. The path passes another small wood and at a corner turns onto a track which is then followed to the road. At the road turn right and follow it south for a short way to the sharp bend round to the left. Here bear right along the track and after 600m take the track on the left alongside the church yard. At the entrance to the churchyard the Angles Way turns right along a fence lined path around a series of properties and grazing fields to the right. The path eventually arrives at the road, turn right over the railway bridge and bear left as the road curves to the east and up to a fork. Bear right along Romany Road and follow it round the slight bend where it then continues straight for 350m. The road then bends 90 degrees to the left and heads north up to the railway line and bends sharply to the right. This road should now be followed in a straight line east, past the viewpoint over Oulton Broad and will eventually arrive at the train station.

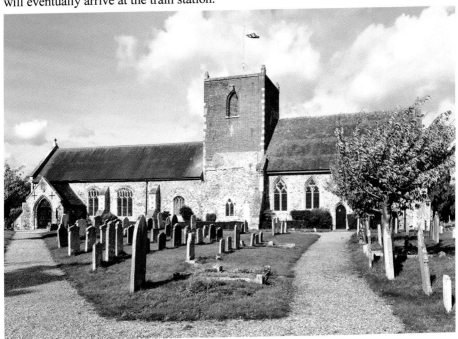

St Michael's Church, Oulton
The interesting church of St Michael in Oulton has clearly had parts rebuilt, restored or changed and added over the centuries. The core of the church is 12th Century and almost certainly Norman making it far older than most other buildings in the local area. What makes this Grade I listed church even more unusual is the central tower which is very rare indeed for the county.

St Olaves

River Waveney

St Olaves

St Olaves is a small village along the River Waveney about equal distance from Great Yarmouth as it is from Lowestoft. The Bell Inn overlooks the staithe by the river and Priory Farm restaurant sits close to the beautiful ruins of St Olaves Priory tucked just off the main road. Close to the many large marinas and about a mile from the village centre is Haddiscoe Railway Station providing frequent links to Norwich and Lowestoft.

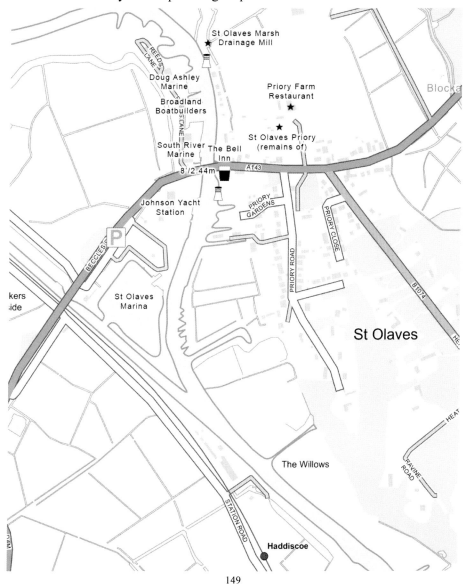

St Olaves Drainage Mill

St Olaves Marsh Drainage Mill is a rare Trestle type mill built in 1910 and later restored in 1980. Due to its rarity and exceptional state of preservation, the mill has been given a Grade II* listing.

Walk 33:

St Olaves Priory & Mill

Distance: 1.2km (0.75 Miles)
Time: 1 Hour
Parking: Roadside

NR31 9HX

From St Olaves free moorings by the drainage mill, follow the footpath on the right behind the riverside properties which sticks to the flood defence wall to the road. Turn left, cross the road and pass The Bell Inn. Just ahead you will notice the entrance to St Olaves Priory Farm and to the left of this is a footpath signposted to St Olaves Priory. Follow the path along the wall to the priory ruins and retrace your steps back to the moorings to finish. Parking for this walk is along a minor road outside the yacht station and marina. Simply head towards the main road and turn right, following the pavement towards the bridge. On the right is a dedicated footbridge towards the Bell Inn where the route can be followed as stated above to the priory ruins.

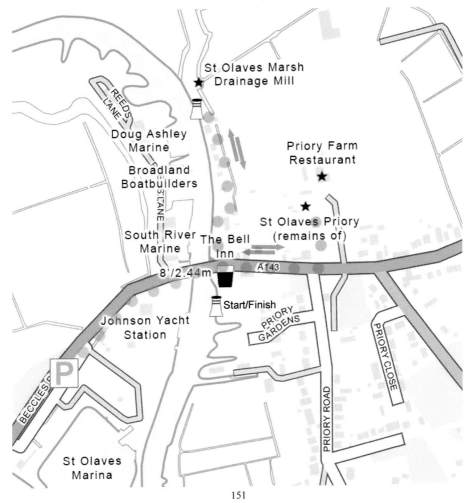

St Olaves Priory Ruins

St Olaves Priory was an Augustinian Priory founded in 1216 close to an ancient crossing of the River Waveney. The Grade I listed ruins are in the care of English Heritage and free to explore, with parts of the Lady Chapel and Refectory visible as well as a superbly preserved early 14th Century undercroft.

Surlingham

River Yare

Surlingham

Surlingham is a picturesque little village on the River Yare near Norwich just north of Rockland St Mary. Mooring is available near the Ferry House Inn and Coldham Hall for customers and free car parking is located just by the parish church of St Mary. The village has a small post office and two pubs, the Ferry House and Coldham Hall, both on the riverbanks of the Yare, one to the north and one to the east. Within the parish is the lovely RSPB Church Marsh nature reserve with short circular walks through the wildlife rich habitat overlooked by the enigmatic ruins of St Saviours Church. Just to the south of the village is the Ted Ellis Nature Reserve which is included in the chapter on Rockland St Mary.

River Yare at Surlingham

RSPB Church Marsh Nature Reserve

RSPB Surlingham Church Marsh Nature Reserve is free to enter and only a short walk from the Ferry House pub or parking area by the church. The reserve is beautiful with stunning views over the small lakes and River Yare with plenty of wildlife to see including the Swallowtail Butterfly and many species of Dragonfly.

From the car park just behind the church, and with the church on your right, follow the track towards the flint cottage. Follow the track on the right alongside the church yard in a straight line for about 320m to the point where it bends sharply left. Just on the right up on a slight hill are the enigmatic ruins of St Saviour's Church which are well worth exploring. To continue the walk head back to the track and turn right to follow it in a straight line for 80m along the field where it then bends sharply round to the right. Continue in a fairly straight line north east past a small shooting range and along the fields until you come out at a road. Turn left at the road and follow it to The Ferry House by the River Yare. Turn left and follow the riverbank along to a gate. Head through the gate and follow the riverside footpath along the Yare for almost 400m until you reach Church Marsh Nature Reserve and a junction in the path. Turn right and follow the path which again runs along the River Yare.

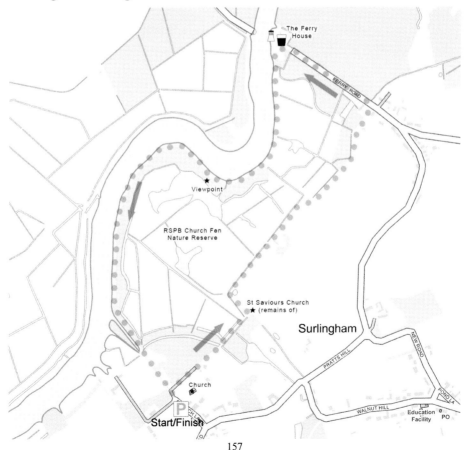

Along this section on the left is a viewpoint which is worth the tiny detour and offers lovely views over the nature reserve. To continue the walk, follow the path along the River Yare to the south west and then away from the river and along a slight incline back up to the church and car park.

St Saviours Church Ruins
The enigmatic ruins of St Saviour's Church overlooking the nearby marshes dates to the 12th Century and the final resting place of local naturalist Ted Ellis who is buried in the graveyard. The church once supported a tower but sadly fell into disrepair and has been out of use since 1705.

Surlingham to Postwick Ferry
The Ferry House is so named because long ago a ferry used to run between the staithe here at Surlingham and Postwick but ceased operation in 1939. The public rights of way still exist today showing its route on the other side of the river.

Broads Authority www.broads-authority.gov.uk	Walking in the Wild www.walkinginthewild.co.uk
Broads National Park Information www.visitthebroads.co.uk	Tour Norfolk Information www.tournorfolk.co.uk
Norfolk Broads Tourism Guide www.norfolkbroads.com	National Rail Enquiries www.nationalrail.co.uk
Long Distance Walkers Association www.ldwa.org.uk	Bus Timetables www.bustimes.org

Noticed something missing or incorrect? Get in touch at walkskyhigh@gmail.com

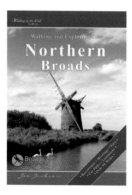
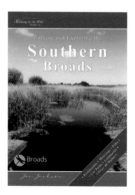

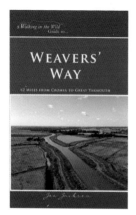
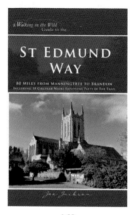